The Energies of Your Life

A unique guide to the subtle invisible energy transactions that affect your every thought, feeling and action.

Sue Zange

Published by Joa's Light, Solihull, West Midlands UK

First published in the UK in 2015 by Joa's Light Limited.
www.joaslight.com | www.energiesofyourlife.com

The author and publisher acknowledge the kind contribution and permission of the people who have provided their personal testimonial or story to support the content of this book.

Images enhanced and developed by Mike Zange. Cover design by Mike Zange. Original base images courtesy of istock.com

(Images in this book are presented in two-dimensional form and are offered only as a conceptual guide to aid understanding of the presence of the human electro-magnetic energy field. In actuality the field is a three-dimensional presence.)

The content of this book is intended to support and increase awareness of an alternative form of healing, therapy and self-management techniques, and provides information and instruction for informational and educational purposes only. The reader should acknowledge and understand that alternative therapies, development exercises or life-style techniques are not a substitute for conventional medicine or the care of medical professional services.

A catalogue record for this book is available from the British Library

ISBN 978-0-9562237-7-7 (Hardback)
ISBN 978-0-9562237-4-6 (Softcover)

Printed and bound in the United Kingdom

This book is produced in Joa's light.

This book is dedicated to the
furtherance of
Humanity Consciousness

To David,
with wishes for
a future of expansive
and joyful days. x
Sue x

Introduction | 1

"We are influenced and sculpted by hidden forces that are beyond our vision or comprehension."

If I told you there was a whole invisible world that you know nothing about, would you be intrigued? Would you want to know more?

What if I told you that what happens in that invisible world affects you, every moment of every day of your life. It influences how you feel, the decisions you make, your perceptions, choices and responses. It drives your creations, influences your actions and affects every thought process you ever have.

Welcome to the World of subtle energy!

I would invite you to embark upon a journey of discovery with me. This journey will offer knowledge, information and insights into the subtle and unseen movements of energy and consciousness that exist invisibly around and within you. The subtle drivers of every aspect of your life.

If someone had said to me at the end of 1997, "Look, within the next two years you are going to acquire an extraordinary set of skills that will give you access to a level of knowledge of which no-one has any full comprehension". Well, I would have laughed that off as fantasy. Who wouldn't laugh that off? But that's how it came to be, and the process led to more than a decade of development and innovation within the realms of subtle energy.

I know from experience that some people encounter in their life a momentous and irrevocable life changing event. I've heard their stories, but I didn't expect one of my own. Back then in 1997, mine was an ordinary life - successful, but ordinary. I was a somewhat shy, lonesome soul, happy raising my children. I was working hard in my business career and that fed me a lot of satisfaction. I was not the extraordinary type. From the outside, nothing about me said 'exceptional talent'.

Writing now, 17 years on from that simplistic view, I have since experienced years of intense discovery and learning in a subject matter that is still uncharted territory and deeply misunderstood by almost the entire population. I have come to know some of the most awesome and inspiring ways of the human being, of life and how it is lived. I have witnessed remarkable change in ordinary people, where just simple adjustments in the flows of their subtle energy environments has brought about the opening of greater potential and the activation of skills and creativity to enrich their lives.

I ask you to join me within the concept of understanding the universe as energy. We know that all things are energy, science shows us that and the laws of physics provide the evidence. For me, subtle energy science has become a way of life and over many years of experience and exploration, I have been able to develop useful techniques which students and clients have successfully applied in their lives.

This book is my way of sharing some of the most vital subtle energy principles with you, offering an awareness that will teach you how to manage the energies of your life more effectively.

We can commence by acknowledging the existence of the human electro-magnetic energy field. Science shows us that this field of energy is present around the human body. In 'alternative' holistic circles people may refer to this as the 'aura'. I always refer to it as the energy field. It is the presence and nature of this field of energy which we are going to explore. This is my area of specialism and I would like to equip you with insight and skills to help you manage and command the flow of these energies on a daily basis. I would like this extraordinary invisible world to become part of your ordinary world, as it has mine.

The ability to sense energy, feel its movement and be aware of subtle 'atmosphere', is becoming more common. Many people are choosing to extend their awareness beyond the known physical, experiencing the sensations of tingling hands, hair raising on arms and shivers down the spine. These are all physical responses to a change in subtle energies and they are common.

This book will guide you through a greater understanding of subtle energies, so that you may come to know some of the more intricate workings of your energy field, the daily energy transactions you are involved with, and the complex energy dynamics you reside within. Most especially, this is your opportunity to discover and understand the relevance and implications of these energies in your everyday life.

My own story of discovery

Since I am inviting you into my world - the world of subtle, invisible energy - you might want to know a little bit more about me. With the abilities of a natural energy sensitive, I have served as an advanced energy field healer since 1999. I have pioneered and developed advanced energy field healing techniques, which have been taught to hundreds of students over the course of 14 years.

I was sensitive to energy as a child, but it was bewildering and tormenting. The energy environment of my childhood was tense, strained and volatile. It made the world a difficult place. I 'knew' things about people, I felt their feelings, their pain, and I could feel their intentions towards others. It was uncomfortable, it was nonsense in my head, it made me emotionally ache. I was young, immature and certainly unable to manage the information and data that my higher sensory abilities brought to me. As a teenager I made a conscious choice not to engage with this acute sensitivity. My choice was to try to 'switch off' these abilities, because they appeared pointless to me at the time. I didn't know at that young age that I had the natural skill of clairsentience (the ability to feel beyond the known physical), or that it was destined to serve some higher value later in life.

It took huge amounts of concerted effort during my adult years to fend off that acute sensitivity. I consciously had to shut out the flow of subtle data that on every possible occasion sought to enter my awareness. I did a good job at keeping it all at bay, having only to be occasionally presented at social events as the 'party-piece'. It would entertain people that I could tell them about the 'ghost' in their house, or read the history of a piece of jewellery or furniture, or tell them things that were happening in their lives. They had great fun with it.

It was at the age of 35, through one of those irrevocable life changing events, that I would discover the power, importance and relevance of the sensory skills and natural abilities that were within me. I experienced severe illness, followed by the trauma of emergency surgery. During the surgery I experienced what I later learned was a 'near death experience'. My understanding of life was changed forever. I could refer to that time as a new awakening upon me. It certainly demanded an acknowledgment and new motivation to create better purpose in my life. That time caused me to shift my perspective about wellness, and the purpose and meaning of physical existence. It led me to seek answers and awareness on a higher and more expansive level, because I had seen and experienced 'things' whilst on the operating table that just had to be explained.

Finding myself confused and traumatised by those events, I felt I had no alternative but to investigate. There was nowhere to find the answers I sought, except 'up there' in that white light space of floating and whispering - the place that had held me in light and then delivered me back to the world. I knew I had heard things, been spoken to. I sensed I had responded.

The illness had left me physically damaged from the major surgery, from infection, from loss of full use of my lungs. I had remained in hospital for seven weeks. I was emotionally distraught and mentally terrorised. For sure, I could not remain that way. I knew I had to heal, I had to be more than a victim of my circumstance.

I realised that if I was going to discover the truth of what happened to me when I was 'in the light', I would need a different level of awareness and sensory ability. So I made the commitment to start learning and reactivating my innate sensitive nature and the dormant skills which lay within me.

It was a speedy process. Within a year I had healed the damage to my body. I had learned energy exercises which strengthened and aligned me and returned my lungs to full breathing capacity. I studied a new healing technique that was just emerging in the UK, which was based on re-energising the flow of the energy field. From that, I discovered I was a natural healer, and I excelled at it. I felt so comfortable when I stood before someone, ready to heal them. It was such a deep sense of rightness and belonging, I felt whole within me. Those were feelings I had never experienced before.

Within one year my higher sensitivity was fully active and fine tuned, such that I could clearly sense others' feelings, needs, intentions, energy imbalance, flows and potentials. Once engaged with another's energy field, I could 'read' and interpret the patterns and forms of energy that resided there. Those energy readings gave me masses of information and data about the emotional state and physical condition of the client. Much to my own amazement, I could also actually see those energy forms and movements with my physical eyes, I had developed the ability of 'energy vision'.

My higher intelligence expanded on all levels bringing me greater knowledge, wisdom and understanding of energy and its movement. Most importantly, I was discovering answers from 'up there', that vast expanse of invisible realms that everyone knows as spirit. It was a complete surprise to me to discover that as your own energy field expands and raises in vibration, it connects to other higher vibrational realms of energy. This higher plane of consciousness offers a level of intelligence and wisdom that can only be described as divine. I was receiving an exquisite education in the nature and way of the human subtle energy system.

Make it useful, make it applicable in life

I have a very practical approach to energy awareness - if it is useful, then we need to make it applicable in life. I'm not interested in just knowing something is there, or just how it works. I want to know how to make things better because of it, how to improve the very substance of every day life because we know something more about how it is operating.

I'm naturally very curious and inquisitive - I enjoy knowledge. In my view, if the universe has found a way to reveal some of its inner workings to me, then I have the absolute right to question and challenge everything that is shown to me or discovered. I have to know, how does this make anything better? What can it do for people? How do I apply it in the world to improve lives?

The first outlet I found for my subtle energy skills was offering healing to clients. In 1999 I commenced full time healing work in my own clinic. I was offered a room to rent in a private doctors surgery and jumped at the opportunity to start my own business. As the clients grew in number I rapidly began to progress and develop intricate techniques for working within the subtle energies of the human electro-magnetic field. At that time, working in the unseen subtle vibrations of the human energy field for the purpose of healing, was very new and relatively unknown in the UK.

The healing clinic soon became very busy with people wanting healing and to know more about this new and revolutionary therapy. The healing potential for clients was extraordinary and they were returning home telling their friends and family, spreading the word of the seemingly magical process that took place when the healer waved their arms about 'in thin air' and cleared and balanced this invisible field.

Don't be fooled into thinking that healing is only for the 'new age' or the 'hippie' stereotypes. My clientele over the years I operated my clinic included business men and women, directors, financiers, entrepreneurs, doctors, the occasional professor, scientists and teachers. I have provided my services to a variety of performers, singers and musicians, and even a few professional footballers.

These people are not fools or fantasists. They attended my healing clinic because it worked, they saw results. They felt better for having their energy cleared, balanced and restructured and their performance and productivity improved as a result. For professional people, taking a couple of hours out of their schedule to attend for energy field healing with me was vital and absolutely worth their time. I had business clients who would arrange flight stopovers at Birmingham Airport as they were travelling across the world, just to spend an hour in the healing clinic with me. There is only one difference between those who attended and you... they discovered the secret that enhanced their well-being. Well perhaps now, with this book, many more of you will discover it.

By 2001 I found myself in demand for public speaking engagements, which was a bizarre transition for someone who had previously been so shy. People, groups and colleges wanting to know more about this new healing method. I was happy to accommodate this, enjoying conveying the knowledge and offering demonstrations and evidence in support of the work. It was a joyous time that was giving me a natural evolvement and growth for my own skills and awareness.

I came to realize that the development of my work was becoming very unique. The rare combination of my natural skills and the aptitude for higher sensory awareness, began to create an extraordinary view of energy, life and consciousness. Over a ten year period of working full time in clinic, I carried out thousands of energy field healing sessions. That's a lot of experience to assimilate, with each case offering deeper insight into the causes and nature of ill-health, wellness, life balance, empowerment and growth. The change and transformation I have witnessed within people has been extraordinary and has shown the amazing capacity within energy to make change.

Subtle energies and most particularly, the human energy field, is my specialist area of expertise. It is a specialism that has been earned through practical application and immense experience. With the ability to see energy flows, I have made the study of invisible subtle energies my passion. This study has produced specialist and advanced techniques for healing through the body's energy field. With the ability to move, clear and transform imbalanced or non-serving energy, I have become highly proficient at helping people manage and transform the energy flows of their lives and regain a sense of well-being.

I began the teaching of Energy Field Healing in 2001, offering techniques that I personally pioneered and developed. It was the only solution to an escalating problem. My clinic was becoming so fully booked that people were waiting many months for an appointment. I couldn't personally accommodate the demand. The answer had to be to train others in the healing techniques I had developed. The benefit gained by hundreds of students over 14 years of teaching, is immense. It is clear that once someone has insight into the way of energy and acquires the skills to manage such energies, life comes into command. This is the primary purpose of sharing this book with you.

I believe you have come to this place for a deeper understanding of the workings of your life. It is my desire to offer such insight to you. I can offer you a level of understanding which will empower you to know more about the energies of your life. Take this opportunity to discover the transactions which hinder or enhance you, and to learn vital ways to assess your state of health and well-being.

The opportunity exists here for you to expand your horizons, to move beyond what you know of the physical world and offer some attention to the higher concepts that are possible, plausible and sensible. My view has always been that we should make this invisible world make sense. We need to know how the knowledge of this can be made applicable in life, such that we can all become better and more well because of it.

Throughout the book you will find genuine statements from people who have been my clients or trained as students with me. These are just a few of the people who have had their lives improved and transformed by subtle energy awareness and the knowledge of how to apply simple techniques to be more well. If life can change for them, then it can change for all of us. Can you imagine a world where all people are more empowered to manage their wellness, their emotional balance, their mindful intent, and the outcome of their own creations? I can.

So take this opportunity to learn, grow and engage with the extraordinary world of subtle energies. A higher level of conscious awareness is evolving for each of us, so this is your opportunity to gain the knowledge you need to grow, enhance and be well.

See Everything as Energy | 2

"The more we learn of subtle fields of energy, the closer we are to peaceful living."

Science tells us that a vibrating field of energy exists within and around all things, that physical matter is mostly 'empty space'. With energy vision, I can tell you that is absolutely so. With energy sensitivity, these fields of energy can be felt, interacted with and transformed by mindful intent.

Once we become open to the concept and possibility of the presence of invisible energies, the obvious question is 'what do we do about it'? Perhaps I can ask you to take a further leap with me and consider that it's possible to interact with these energies in such a way as to make a difference to their flow and essence.

If all things are energy, then as humans we are constantly transmitting and receiving energetic flows and transactions. Our thoughts, our feelings, our actions and intentions, exists as an energy flow, a resonance. The purpose and essence of these flows are dictated by our desires and intentions.

When you say something, you intend to convey that communication for a purpose. The intention of that purpose literally carries the energy of that communication to those you are speaking to.

When you feel something, the essence of that feeling and emotion radiates outwards from your body and the energy of such emotion is felt on a subtle level by those around you. Hence, you can sense and empathise with someone's feelings, you can share in their emotion, you can respond to their feelings. With every movement of our physical body, we generate a transmission of energy, our body responding to the intent of our mind to take certain action.

Multiple Streams of Subtle Energy Data

Now put all those aspects together and consider the immense amount of alternating flows of energy which are occurring every moment of the day for you. As you think, calculate, speak, listen, feel, consider, act and respond, masses of energy data is being processed and assimilated by you. Multiple data streams are entering through your known physical senses, complemented and enhanced by all the subtle energy data received by your higher senses. This is intelligence in action.

That simple awareness - the presence of energy transactions - needs to be the starting point of your understanding of subtle energy. From the moment you realise these invisible streams of data are pouring out of you into the world, you will comprehend that you are a contributor to the lives of others. In addition, once you recognise that you are receiving the subtle transactions of others and that such energies are absorbing into your own field of energy, then your view of who you engage with changes up a gear, to a different level of awareness.

Once you become aware and apply focus to these transactions and energy flows, you can empower yourself within a whole new realm of operational living - within a field of higher intelligence. Alternative choices and outcomes become possible, known and available. New potentials to change the quality of your life will enter your awareness, such that you may improve those aspects of living which are important to you.

So, from this point on, view your thoughts as energy flows which you transmit out into the world, which you direct towards other people, and which drive your life's intention. Stop for a moment and consider... what is the quality and nature of the thoughts you have? Do they enhance the quality of your life, or do they lessen it? Are they supportive of others or detrimental to them? Just by thinking of someone or something, you are connecting through subtle energy flows. What effect are you having? What contribution are you making?

Imagine now all your feelings and emotions as an energy wave, moving around and within you, and then radiating out into the world... touching others. At any given moment you are a mass of bubbling, or simmering, emotional compulsion that is yearning to find expression in the world. Every single thing you do is driven by an underlying feeling. Everything.

So how are you feeling? Are the emotional energies that you transmit to others generally good, supportive, buoyant? Are you offering love and care, attention and kindness? Are you joyful and happy to be engaged in your daily life activities? Do you consider that you bring well-serving and positive feeling energies to your interactions with others?

Or are you often low, miserable, wounded or vengeful, and transmitting that out to others? Do words come out of you with hostility or spite? Is there a simmering anger or pain within you that is just waiting to burst out upon the world? What is the quality and nature of the feelings you generally transmit out to the world on a regular basis?

Once you start to view your state of being as a flow of energy transactions, your awareness will change. You come to realise how you are creating and affecting life - people, relationships, situations, future potentials. Your self-understanding will grow and you will begin to see the nature of who you are and why you behave the way you do. Such awareness will ask you to take a good look at how you contribute to life, or indeed, how you consume it. For in subtle energy there are only two states of flow - either you are contributing and enhancing the greater good of all, or you are consuming and diminishing it.

That's one of the primary empowering principles of understanding subtle energy. We can all learn how to manage our lives differently, to make change where needed and to create and enhance the aspects of life that we enjoy and value.

Such greater awareness will also help you realise how others are affecting you! Gaining insight to how others influence your life and what they bring to you as contribution, will create a major shift in who you choose to share time and invest your future with. You will be able to make clearer choices about what serves your well-being and that of others, in regard to your daily people interactions.

The energies of life are flowing around you and through you, constantly. You are receiving and transmitting, constantly. That means you are always affecting others with the outflow of your energy intent and you are constantly affected by the energies you receive from them. Once you acknowledge that, it will motivate you to take a deeper look at the quality and value of those incoming and outgoing energy transactions. Such consideration will bring you to a clearer understanding of what is important and valuable to you in life, and what is not.

The busier your life becomes, the more energy transactions you are dealing with - incoming and outgoing. Each and every one of us has our own 'energetic capacity', that is, how much energy traffic can flow through our energy system before it becomes overloaded or imbalanced. Once your energy system exceeds its capacity to handle and process the data of those transactions, your system will enter a state of overload and stress.

An overload and stress situation in the energy will most certainly present physical stress in your life. Your energy and mindful processes will begin to try to process the backlog, which will slow you down and put you out of natural sequence. You will lose the ability to concentrate and your memory recall will lessen. An overload in the energy system will create disorder, because you are 'over capacity'. Life consequences will then occur. Later in these chapters, we will look at the consequences of being energetically overloaded and stressed. Once the energy system becomes imbalanced and 'out of flow' it will cause profound effects on your health, productivity, creativity and state of well-being.

Gain insight and understanding to improve your life

Subtle energy awareness allows you insight into the truth of matters. It gives intuitive sense which is not available through the physical senses of the manifest world. As an awareness is developed of how subtle energies are initiated, progressed and concluded, you will come to understand the natural sequence and positioning of life's happenings.

Your new understanding will also help you to see interfering energies and most importantly, which aspects of life are serving you well and which are not. This is a life empowerment process which subtle energy awareness initiates.

What I am offering is an enrichment process. It is a way of understanding the invisible and intangible aspects of life which drive your potentials, affect your actions, influence all incoming occurrences and drive all outgoing intentions. Most importantly, it will help you to understand the 'why' and 'how' life circumstances occur and their effect upon you.

From years of experience, I can tell you that once you have insight into the way of subtle energies and develop some skills to manage such energy flows, life will come into your own command. For now though, let's take a look at your energy system as a whole, so you can begin to learn how to understand your own state of being, through 'energy eyes'.

"I have been privileged to know and train with Sue for more than ten years. During this time, my life has greatly changed for the better, as I have grown in becoming aware of the human energy field and the subtle energies around us. Sue has trained me, and many others, in simple energy management techniques and principles that continuously help me manage my life. It has made a huge difference to my life. A greater sense of awareness, well-being and love enveloped my life from the very first training session. All the courses have inspired me to be greater and better in supporting humanity.

There is no greater gift than awareness. As a therapist, I am honoured to be able to support clients through using Energy Field Healing and have seen real results, almost immediately. As a Mother, I have been able to support my children and grandchildren with their energy and have a greater understanding of their needs. As an individual, I am able to use these daily principles to enhance my life and make a real difference to those around me.

The principles of subtle energy that Sue has taught me will forever remain the cornerstones of my life. One day, these techniques will be used in everyone's daily lives. Then the world will truly be a better place."

C Lyon, Commercial Property Marketing Executive,
Advanced Energy Field Healer & Meditation Teacher

The Human Energy Field | 3

"We know that all things are energy. So... where is it, how does it flow, and what is its relevance?"

The human energy field is an electro-magnetic field of energy which emanates from the core centre of the human body. I have made the study of the human energy field my passion. My acute higher sensitivity allows me to feel the fine layers of energy of the subtle field and the intricacies of energy forms and patterns that reside there. As a specialist energy field healer, I have the ability to move, clear and transform imbalanced or non-serving energy. I have become highly proficient at helping people manage and change their energy flows.

This field of energy flows throughout the internal physical body and generally radiates outward from the body approximately 60-80 centimetres. People who have strong energy flow, who are emotionally stable and mentally clear, have a much stronger radiance of energy. Their field may be well in excess of one metre in radius from the physical body. Their energy presence is strong, and people around them will feel the power of such presence.

The opposite is also true. A person who is unwell, stressed, fatigued, debilitated, or suffering with physical illness, will have much less strength and flow in their field. Their presence is weak. I have worked with clients whose energy felt almost nonexistent it was so weak and they have had to have their field completely structurally rebuilt. Everyone's subtle sense is able to detect when someone's field is weak and you will most likely find yourself enquiring about their wellness. Detecting another's weakness or strength is part of our intuitive and instinctive senses and we respond accordingly.

On a general basis though, most people will 'contain' their energy to about 60 centimetres, so that they live a 'contained' and manageable life. This is how we 'hold' our own space and this containment acts as a boundary by which we keep unwelcome people away from our inner space. Psychologists refer to this as 'personal space' and actually, it is an energetic boundary.

The boundary of the field creates the capacity of the field. Therefore, those with weak energy will be able to cope with far fewer energy transactions than those with a strong and buoyant field. Stronger and more radiant energy field equals greater capacity for life.

Our energy radiance expands or contracts with our activities

The layers of the field and its 'containment' boundary do not remain static. We open and expand our energies when we are with people we enjoy, care for, trust, love or feel shared connection with. On those occasions our energy naturally radiates outwards to connect to them, because we trust that we are safe in their presence and we are enjoying being together. We want to be with that person. So when we are comfortable we 'open up' to share our presence with them. The two energy fields 'engage' with each other, share presence and feed energy resource to each other.

The opposite is also true. If we feel threatened, anxious, unsafe, bewildered or confused by another, we withdraw our energies inwards and 'contain' ourselves more securely. These are the scenarios when we do not trust the actions or intent of the other person and therefore instinctively protect our own presence. We energetically reinforce the boundary and intentionally try to separate from that person. Mentally, we become on alert or on-guard, and may start to look for indications that confirm what we are sensing on the subtle level. Emotionally, we withdraw to ensure we offer no vulnerability, until we have assessed the threat level and analysed an acceptable response or course of action. It's an intelligent function which takes place on a subtle level. You might recognise this as times when you just don't connect with someone and you may find yourself unreasonably suspicious of their intentions or actions. Can you recall times you've thought 'I don't know, there's just something about them that doesn't feel right'?

For those who have endured severe wounds or traumas in life the inwardly contained, protected state becomes inherent. Without even realising, people shut themselves off from the energy transactions of the world in order to remain safe from pain or threat. They try to be more protected from future emotional wounds. However, this may also mean they will be limited in receiving the potentials of goodness, joy and happiness - the greater opportunities that life may bring. When we withdraw from the outer world, we become locked in our inner world and the natural flow of life energies becomes limited and constrained by the presence of the energetic barriers.

It is common to see people in an energetically 'contained' or withdrawn state. It is nature. When we are feeling stressed or unsafe, we retreat. For some, there has never come a point when safety has been reinstated and so they live habitually in a withdrawn state.

Throughout the many years of offering service in energy field healing, my experience of transforming the energetic state from 'contained' to 'expansive' has been immense. One of the primary objectives of energy field healing is to create an energetic environment whereby people can return to their true, relaxed, openly joyful nature.

The Structure of your Energy Field

In order for the energy field to become radiant and strong, it requires certain aspects to be present. Firstly, its primary central flow has to be stable and balanced. The human electro-magnetic field has a main central axis (channel) which runs vertically through the centre of the body. I will always refer to this as the 'central channel'. All other aspects of the energy system flow into, or outwards from this central axis.

Secondly, the field needs all its many layers of resonance (its outward radiance) to be clear and resonating at as high a vibration as is possible for that person. The vibration (resonance) of the energy field is affected by the emotional and mental energy 'forms' and 'patterns' that are present within it. I call this the 'current energetic state'. I shall explain more on that as we move through the book, because the first point of understanding your energy is to know how to recognise and assess your current energetic state.

Thirdly, the energy field requires a continual supply of fresh source energy to maintain and sustain its functions. The field draws in fresh natural resources of universal energy in two key places. Firstly, from the ground (Earth energy), drawing in a supply from nature. Secondly, from above the head, commonly referred to as the 'crown', where it draws in higher frequencies of energy, referred to as 'sky' or 'cosmic' energies.

The two parts of the energy field which naturally draw in source energies must be clear, open and functioning correctly. If the access points for drawing in source energy are not flowing correctly, people can become dependent upon the alternative of drawing their resources from other people. If you have people around you who you find draining to be with, it is possible they are consuming some of your energy as you 'engage' with them, because they are in need.

It is the access points of the field which become lessened or even blocked, when someone withdraws and inwardly 'contains' their field. As I explained earlier, this can occur when someone is in pain or distress, in fear or feeling vulnerable. In such a state, not only does the outside world get 'shut out', but the inner world also becomes diminished, due to an inability to connect to fresh flowing outer energy sources. **Picture 1** shows you the central channel of energy and

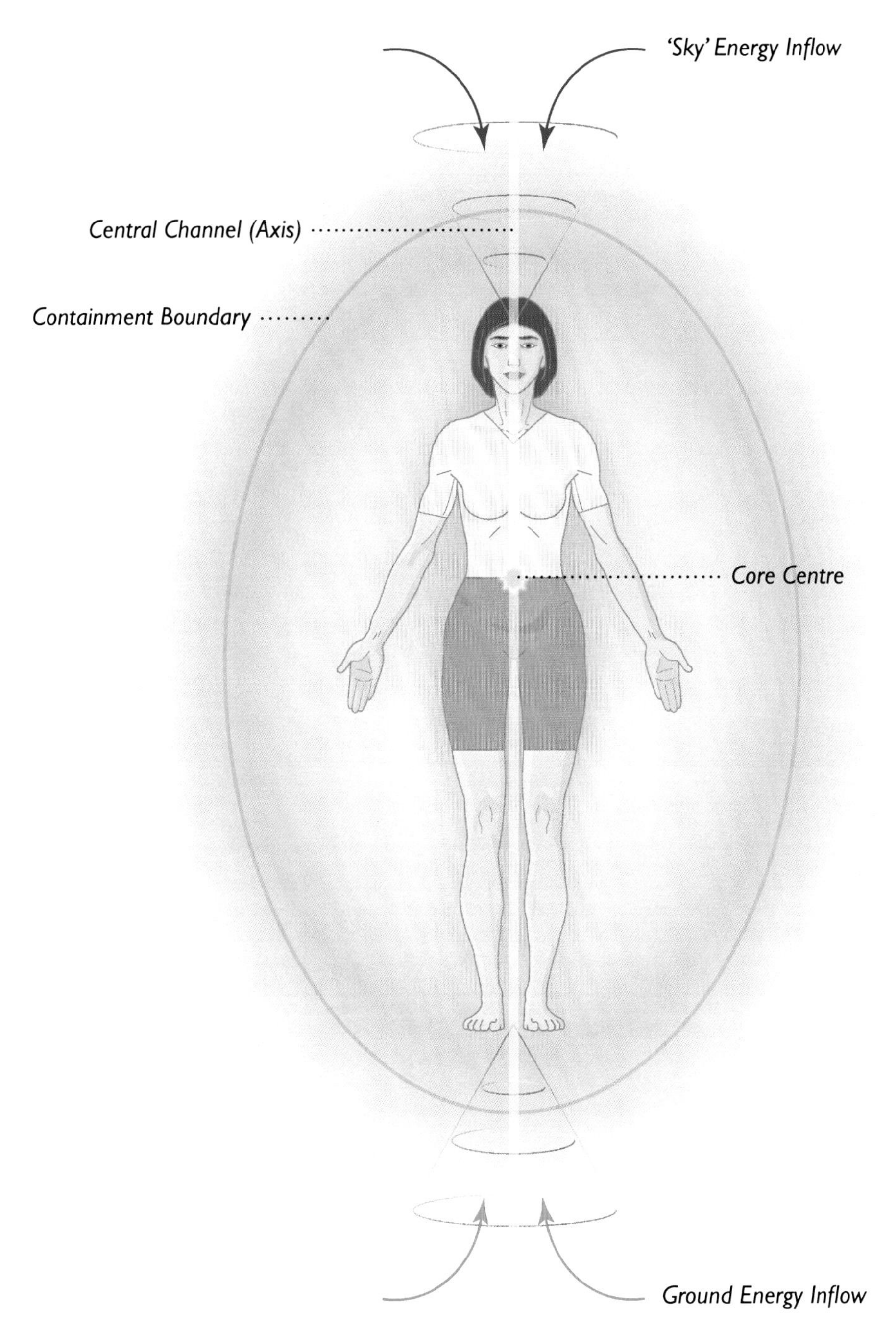

Picture 1 - Structure Of The Energy Field

how natural source energies enter both at the top and the bottom. Your core centre point, is the energy field's structural centre and its place of optimum stability. It is this point that is being referred to when we say you are 'centred'.

This field of energy, which traditionally has been referred to as an 'aura', radiates out from the core centre of your physical body and the main central channel (axis). As the field radiates outwards the energies become finer in resonance and higher in frequency, and it presents as different 'layers' of energy. When we feel these with our hands, the layers close to the body are more dense and with more substance than the layers at say, one metre radius from the body. The outermost layers feel like soft fine gossamer threads when the field is balanced and clear. In such a clear state, the hand moves through all the layers in a silken softness. A well cleansed and balanced energy field feels light and softly flowing, having had any dense energy forms released or transformed by the healer.

The energy layer closest to the physical body is the most dense in resonance. This layer is only one level up in energy frequency from the physical body and is therefore the easiest to sense or 'see'.

Coming outward from the body through different layers of subtle energy resonance, you would reach the point of containment I mentioned earlier. In the field, this layer of energy actually feels bouncy like applying gentle pressure to the surface of an inflated balloon. It is an energetic boundary. When teaching my students, they are all hugely entertained by feeling the presence of that 'bouncy boundary'. It creates a profound shift in their perspective when they realise they are feeling something on their physical hand which actually exists in the invisible space some 50-60 cm from the body.

Continuing further out away from the body and beyond the containment boundary, the energies are finer and lighter. People sometimes refer to this as 'higher self' or 'soul energies'. Indeed, the energies at this outer level are very high in frequency and relate to the higher frequency feelings of love, joy, compassion and kindness. Someone who is open, joyous and lovingly involved with life, will have an expansive and radiant energy field and will therefore, be more engaged with their higher energies.

I think it's particularly important to understand that the higher frequencies of love, joy and compassion are abundantly accessible in the outermost layers of the field and they filter inwards to sustain our physical presence. It is therefore in our best interest for our own wellness and enjoyment of life that we do not 'contain' or limit the openness of our field. If we do, then we are limiting our access to those higher aspects of joyous living.

When I mention different frequencies of energy, I am referring to different speeds and amplitudes of energy waves. The best way to describe it is to imagine an old-fashioned radio, where you move the control and it passes through different frequency bands and you get to hear short bursts from different radio stations. Energy exists like that - various bands of different resonances.

So as we move further away from the more dense energies of the physical body, the energy becomes lighter and finer. The real secret to a strong and balanced energy field is gaining 'cohesion' between all the different layers. Balanced energy is cohesive, meaning, all aspects of the field are fully inter-connected and co-operating with each other.

An electro-magnetic field... it's electrical and magnetic

The human energy field is electro-magnetic. It comprises electrical pulses and waves and magnetic waves and flows.

The magnetism within the field is the means by which you attract other energetic aspects into your life - people, opportunities, prosperity and so on. Magnetism within the field is the energy of feelings and emotions. All attraction is a product of feelings, desires and emotions. If you allow your feelings to flow outward, they will naturally attract a matching energetic resonance. Therefore the nature and essence of the type of feelings you experience dictates the quality of what, or who, flows into your life.

The electrical flow throughout the field is intelligent processing - thought patterns, sequencing, logic, intentions, natural electrical impulses for instructing the body's functions and systems. In energy terms I refer to these aspects as 'mental' - of the mind. Mental energies carry intent, purpose, programming instructions, intelligence processing and memory patterns.

As a human being, you are nurtured by the flows of the natural energies around you. Your energetic system is designed for planet Earth. The radiations of ground energies that emanate upwards from the surface of the planet and its nature kingdoms feed into your electro-magnetic field and energise you with frequencies of energy essential to the sustenance of physical life.

You are further fuelled by the cosmic energies (higher frequencies) that flow into the Earth from off-planet, sources such as the sun's radiation and cosmic energy waves. The combination of the earthbound energy frequencies flowing into your field, together with the universal higher energies, gives you a flow of natural source by which you function and survive. The reason we generally feel better when we are out in nature and absorbing source energies is because it feeds our subtle energy system.

Spiralling vortexes of energy which transmit and receive

In addition to the natural flows of source energy creating radiance in the energy field, there is a vertical array of energy centres which are receiving, processing and transmitting energies throughout the field. **Picture 2** shows the energy centres that are most relevant to the flow, structure and balance of the human energy field.

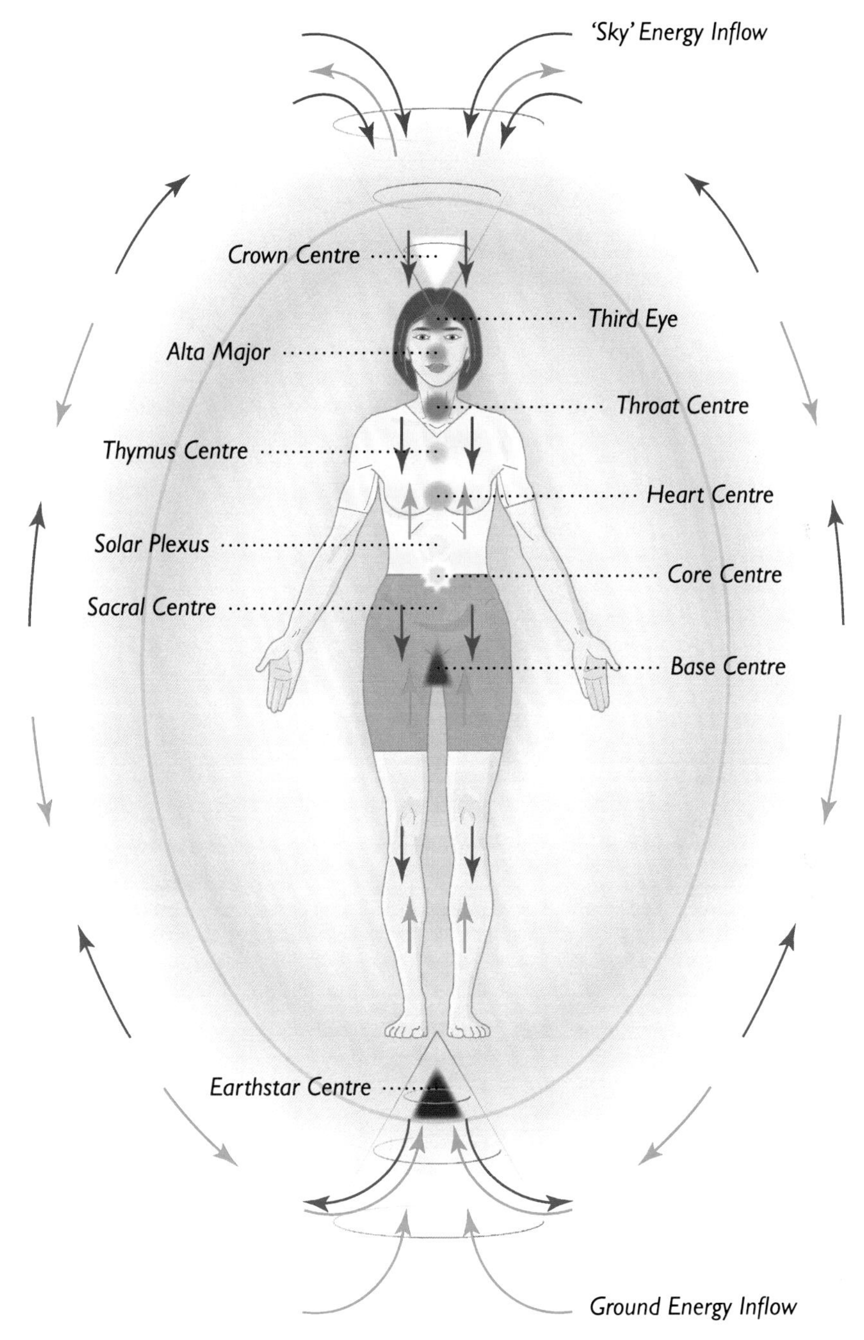

Picture 2 - Natural Two-Way Flow of Energies and the Energy Centres

Emanating from the central channel (axis) of energy which runs vertically through your body, these spiralling vortexes of energy serve the function of transmitting and receiving life's energy transactions. These vortexes have traditionally been referred to as 'chakras'. In more modern terms, we now call them energy centres.

The energy centres (chakras) are minute at their point of origination and/or culmination within the central channel. At the point they expand out and reach the surface of the skin, they are approximately 6-8 cm in diameter. Upon reaching the first layer of subtle energy surrounding the physical body (just 3-5 centimetres from the surface of the skin) they are approximately 8-10 cm in diameter. Again, this is only an approximation, because the stronger a person's energy field, the wider and more powerful the energy centre. The opposite is also true, in a person who is unwell, stressed, tired or debilitated, the energy centre is smaller in diameter.

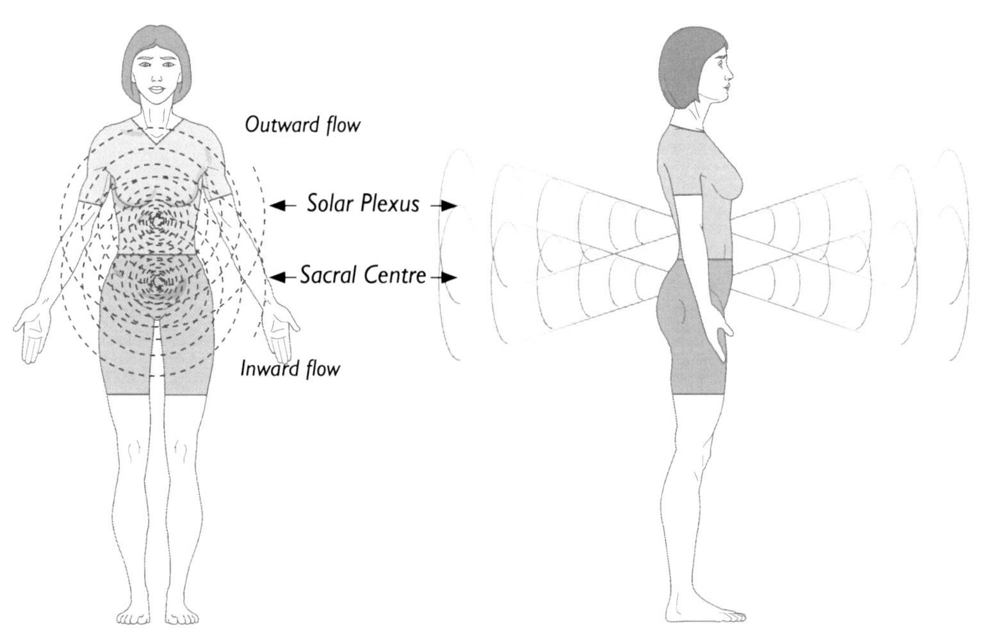

Picture 3A - Example of Energy Centre flows on front and back of body

The flow of the energy centres spirals in two alternate directions - outwards from the body, which is your radiance and transmission out into the World and inwards into the body, receiving the external energies from your involvement with others, situations and life events. These cone-shaped, spiralling vortexes (shown in Picture 3A) are constantly streaming subtle energy data.

Picture 3B - The Flow of the Energy Centres creating 'presence'

In their outward flow the energy centres expand proportionately as they progress through the layers of the field. Therefore at the point they reach the outermost layers they have widened considerably and the content and essence of the energies they are carrying, forms a major part of the field's energy resonance and radiation - your presence.

Picture 3B is only offered to give a concept of how the energy centres flow outwards and inwards within the field. The powerful flow of these vortexes of energy can only clearly be defined by the hand, close to the body and up to about 30 cm outwards in the field. Beyond that, the spiralling energies blend into the flow of the layers of the field and become indistinct from aspects of the moving energy transactions and forms.

When training my students to feel and sense the energy field with their hands, their first practise is always close to the body. In the first energy layer, just 3-5 cm from the body, the flow of the energy centres is quite easily detected and it is the students' first experience of different 'types' of subtle sensory data. Energy centres can be energetically blocked, dense, 'sharp', structurally damaged, 'hot' or 'cold' and these indications of imbalance within the centre offer good practise for the trainee healers.

Just as the layers of the energy field differ in resonance (energy frequency), so too do the energy centres. They are positioned vertically upon the main central channel of energy and the closer they are to the Earth energy, the lower the frequency of energy within that centre. That's important to understand because each energy centre aligns to a different band of energy frequencies. As such, they receive or transmit different types of energy essence.

The heart centre, for example, will receive and transmit different energies to say, the sacral centre, which is in the middle of the abdomen. In this way, each centre serves a specific purpose within the subtle energy system in terms of facilitating your experiences of varied feelings, intents and actions. Some centres will primarily process mental energies, others process the energies of emotions.

As we continue through the chapters of this book, I will offer you more insight and knowledge about energy centres (chakras), the layers of the field, and how to manage your mental and emotional resonances. But first, let's explore the vital nature of magnetism because it is the driving power by which all things are created.

Your Core Feeling | 4

"The ultimate goal of emotional understanding is authentic living... the ability to be true to yourself."

Our primary nature is feeling. We are naturally driven by love... the need and desire to express love and receive love. That means at our very core, we are feeling beings. We feel first, then we think. I know there are many who would state that we think first, but that is not true. As an experienced and skilled energy sensitive, I can assure you that we feel first. The subtle intelligent data received on a raw feeling level occurs first.

As human animals, we have instinct. In times of immediate threat or need, our instincts activate. This is our base genetic programming that we come into life with. An instinctive response bypasses the need for a logical thinking process. It activates purely in response to a feeling, not a thought.

A common example of that would be the 'fight or flight' reflex - an instinct that activates with immediacy upon threat to life. We feel the danger and we react instinctively. We FEEL the danger. There isn't time to gather information, analyse, and construct a thought out response. Our instincts are coded within our core, and our core is that of feeling. It's primary, visceral and hardwired into our instinctive genetic programming.

You will know this for yourself. If you have ever acted out of instinct, ever just taken reflex action to something, you will know that afterwards you cannot recall pre-thinking about what you did. There was no thought. You felt something, you reacted instinctively. I had an occurrence of this when I was young, just about 12 years old. I was sitting one afternoon on the steps outside our building. Suddenly, there was a huge explosion. My next conscious thought was about what the explosion could have been, but by then I was actually some 30 metres away behind the building. I had fled. Getting my thoughts together, I walked around the building to see what the explosion was and I saw others doing the same. It was a mains gas pipe and it had exploded just 50 metres or so from where I had been sitting. I'm sure at some point in life, you also have experienced an instinctive response and have come to know that such action does not occur from thought.

If we can come to understand that our primary nature is that of feeling, then our view of our life experiences and circumstances can be seen through different eyes. There is the tiniest amount of time, nanoseconds, before an initial feeling transmits data to the mind. It is in those few moments that the feeling is in its pure form, magnetism. Once the data reaches the mind, it becomes transmuted into a thought process, electrical. The mind takes the subtle energy data it receives and processes it, in order to find purpose and meaning within it. However, the original energy 'form' of the feeling will still exist. Our feelings reside in the field as energy flows and forms. They remain until such time as we find that meaning, grow and enhance because of it, and then generate an onward flow for that energy. When it has served its purpose, we release it.

The manner by which you deal with subtle energy data depends on your personal character and philosophy. If you are mentally alert and focused, then without awareness training, you may never notice the moment it takes to transfer a feeling into a thought process. It occurs automatically. Any experience will turn quickly into mental processing and the original essence of the feeling will just 'pass you by', as though it never existed. Without awareness, a thought process may then possibly suppress or negate the nature and essence of any feeling. As such, you will not generally relate to your feelings and so their forms and patterns will remain in your field, waiting for an opportunity to express.

If you are just a fraction slower with the application of your mental intelligence, then you will have a few seconds of 'suspension' in the feeling, before it moves into a thought process. In that scenario, you are likely to have more awareness of the original feeling and if necessary, you will easily be able to re-connect to the feeling at a later stage by directing your focus into it. That means you will always have the opportunity to explore and engage with your feelings and enjoy the richness of experience that it can bring to you. It also means that you may be willing to fully engage with the feeling at the time it is occurring, which again, will offer you a deeper richness to the experience of life.

Wondering which type you are? The alert and mentally focused are the ones who possibly miss out on the emotional essence of life's transactions. They may be 'stuck in their head' and will invest primarily in the logical thinking process. They may find it difficult to engage with emotions and would purposely have to work their way towards identifying the feeling. As a positive, such 'thinkers' are great planners, strategists and analysts - creation needs a plan.

If you're one who responds just a fraction slower, then in highly charged situations, for example an argument, you are likely to find yourself unable to speedily deliver a clear and thought out response. This is because the impact of the feeling has 'knocked' you. A little later, you'll be asking yourself why you didn't say this, or that, or think quickly enough to respond differently. Recognise that? In such situations, you are one who needs the energetic impact of the feeling to be managed or lessened in order to respond. However, it also means that when you are in loving and joyous states, you will be fully engaged with the splendour and happiness that creates and experience them fully.

I am somewhat generalising here because of course there are a multitude of ways that each and every one of us would deal with different circumstances and situations. I offer this two-type distinction just to explain a general norm as a subtle energy observation in relation to feeling and thinking.

With awareness... there is another option

The true purpose of subtle energy understanding is to engage in the process of life as a whole. At that first point of feeling, you can be with that feeling fully, to experience it in its true nature. If you can be bold and willing to experience feelings without fear or suppression, then you can experience life situations fully as they occur. That surely, is the fullest potential by which we can live any experience. By remaining with the feeling, we do not allow the mind to rapidly convert it to a mental process. A willingness to fully engage with a feeling will leave available the processing space the mind needs to formulate an accurate and clear intelligent response.

The most common reason many do not engage with the feeling, is that some feelings are not pleasant or enjoyable. If you have a history of emotional wound or trauma, then your intelligence will have set up a system by which feelings can be bypassed quickly in order to ensure you are not hurt further. Our nature is to try to protect ourselves and by doing so, we may limit our life experience. I would ask you not to condemn that protective process, it is part of our nature and an important aspect of survival programming. It is a higher intelligence function which if understood and commanded correctly in life, will serve its purpose well. Without being commanded, the protective function will run in 'default' mode and will have control of your life whether you realise it or not.

In order to experience the broadest potential of life, we need to accept that we will encounter pain as well as joy, despair as well as love, difficulty as well as ease. That's life, it happens to us. Sometimes disproportionately, but inevitably.

We can choose to manage our lives in a 'safe' way, running in protected mode, whereby we avoid, ignore or suppress the feelings. Or alternatively, we can be bold and endeavour to feel the richness of life in whatever form it presents and engage ourselves fully in the feelings of being alive. Let's understand how this is relevant in energy terms.

On a daily basis... how do you generally feel? Can you clearly identify and name the feelings? Do you generalise, with descriptions such as 'low', 'flat', 'okay', 'so so', 'fine'. On any given day, do you consider the majority of your feelings are good, joyous, nice, happy, enriching? Or are they often miserable, angry, vengeful, spiteful or destructive feelings? Perhaps you are emotionally flat-lining, with a general feeling of boredom and mediocrity?

The reason I ask you to identify this, is because each feeling is a specific energetic resonance. An energy form or pattern exists within your energy system for every feeling you experience. So whether you consciously acknowledge it or not, the feeling is there. You cannot just run away from your feelings, they are live and present within your subtle energy system. The subtle energy forms of feelings remain in the field until they are acknowledged, processed, learned from and released. That's the process of how we grow as human beings.

Now, if the majority of your feelings and emotions are high quality, feel-good times, then you are doing well. You are likely to be enjoying your life, managing experiences that are challenging and keeping yourself emotionally stable and balanced. Such energy resonance will strengthen your energy system and keep your field buoyant and light.

However if you're feeling the heavier, bring-you-down emotions more often than you can manage or would wish, then your energy is holding resonance which diminishes you. In the energy system, non-serving feelings are dense and slow. They restrict the flow of purposeful energy and they limit the lightness and joy that can be present in your life.

If we look at this through 'subtle energy eyes' we see that the tone and essence of all feelings existing within your energy system, are affecting all incoming and outgoing transmissions. The energy resonance within your field is the filter of your life. If your feelings are high energy resonance, then their effect on daily activity will be positive. However, if the energy forms are slow and dense in resonance because they originate from troubled feelings, then they will adversely affect your ability to view your life perspectives and potentials with clarity or legitimacy. Such energy forms will cloud your ability to positively apply yourself in life and will limit your capacity to feel good.

The resonance of all energy forms in your field creates a filter of perspective through which you experience the World (Picture 4).

How you feel about things is your primary driver in life

Have you contemplated recently how you feel? More importantly, have you considered why you feel this way? From an energy perspective, we have two things to consider:

1. The nature of the existing energy forms of feelings and emotions that have built up in your energy system over your life's experience. This includes all past trauma, difficulties, pain and distress - generally termed 'baggage'.

2. The degree of influence that such pre-existing energy forms have upon any new feelings and potentials that are arising in current life experience. Every new situation, every moment of thought or deliberation, every action and choice, is influenced by the pre-existing energetic state.

Have you experienced that scenario where something happy occurs and you find yourself momentarily fully in the enjoyment of that, but a short time later feeling a sense of futility that the good feeling won't last and everything will just revert to the 'usual' way of feeling? And it does!

In energy terms, that's a clear example of your desire to enjoy the moment, feeling it and then as the energy transaction moves through your field it becomes 'contaminated' by the presence of other pre-existing non-serving energy forms.

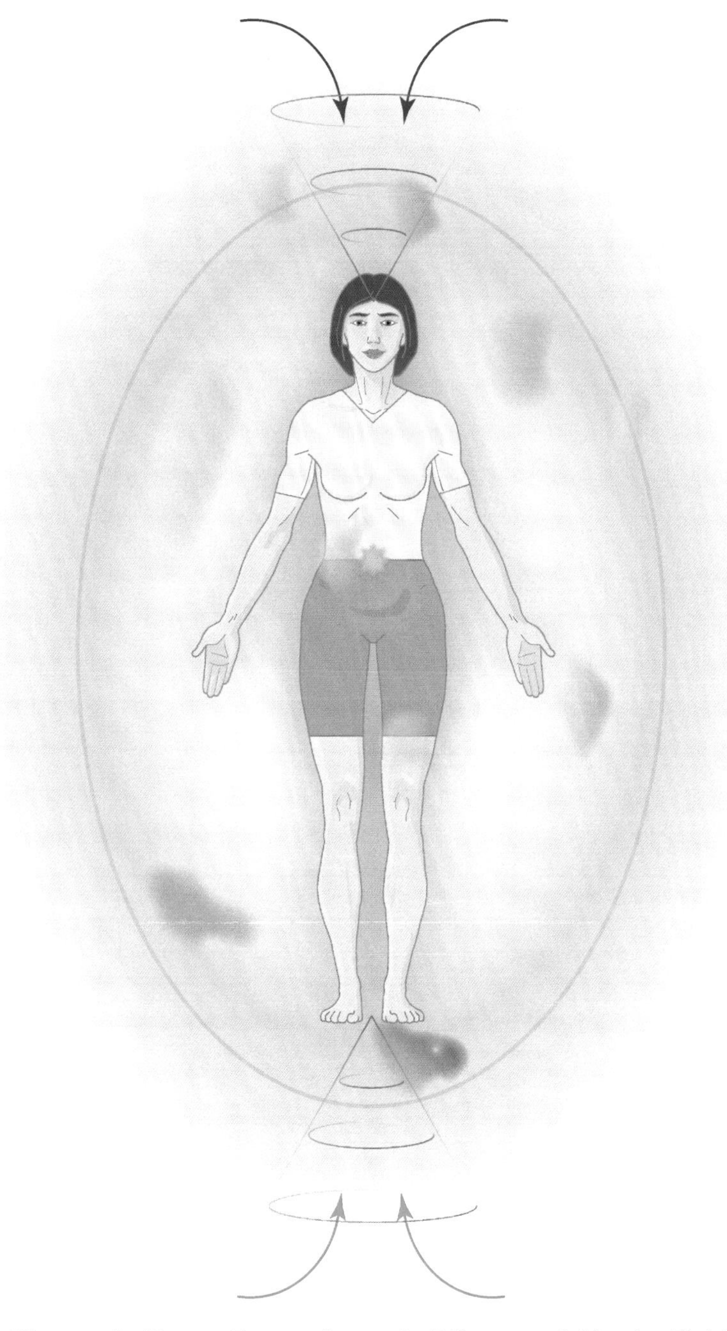

Picture 4 - Dense Energy forms building up within the Field

When I refer to 'non-serving', I mean any element which does not support your happiness and well-being. In life we endeavour to engage in experience that supports us in being the true expression of our inner love. I call this serving, meaning it serves your higher nature. We also sometimes engage in experience that lessens the virtue of our true nature, such activity harms our well-being. I call this non-serving.

Consider the possibility that your pre-existing energetic state may be robbing you of the higher potential of the next moment!

Our feelings reside between two extremes of the energy frequency spectrum. At one end, the highest, fastest frequency energy we experience is that of love. At the opposite end, the slowest and lowest frequency is that of fear. Fear is the most dense and slow energy resonance within the human subtle energy system.

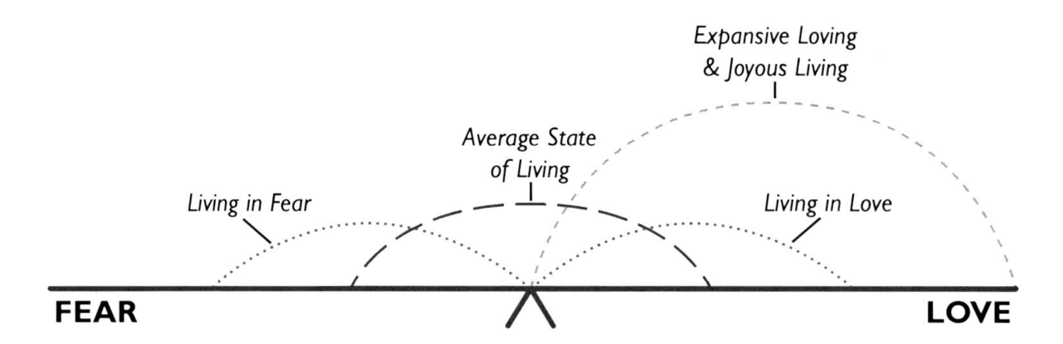

Picture 5 - The Love / Fear Energy Spectrum

We live each day anywhere between those two extremes - hopefully, more in love than fear. It is inevitable that at some time, life will present us with experience akin to the lower, denser part of the energy spectrum. These energies will enter our energetic system and we will either process and release them, or we will hold onto them.

Holding on and holding back? Or letting go and moving on?

An overly-protected and contained energy system will hold on to experiences. It has to, it has no automatic outflow, it is contained. Alternatively, an open and flowing energy system will learn and grow from an experience and then release those energy traces. Put simply, it's either about letting go and moving on, or holding on and holding back. I know what you would prefer as your first choice.

Feelings occur with every life experience. In the subtle field, the energies of circumstances, situations and people are received by you, they will then combine with your inner nature and character, and produce feelings. This is 'how you feel' about something and it's the primary driver of your response. I am asking you to consider the possibility that 'how you feel' about something may not be true or pure to your inner nature, because it has been filtered through the complexity of the energy forms and patterns pre-existing in your field. How clear is your field? Because if it isn't clear, then it is bearing influence upon every experience that is occurring for you.

I would ask you to bear in mind that you are the sum of all the feelings, of all the experience, you have ever encountered. Wherever you have held on to an emotion, it's energy form will be residing within you - in the body, or around you in the field. Your emotional presence and whatever energy resonance it holds, will influence every other feeling and response to feeling, that you encounter. The more clear you are of old emotions, the more empowered you are to live a clear and emotionally unencumbered life.

Emotional energies reside in the energy field as colour. They look like swirls and movements of colour, or like coloured 'clouds'. When these are the energies of painful or distressed feelings the colours within the field appear dull, even grey. People lose their brightness when they experience dense emotions. However, when emotions are light and joyous, the colours become vibrant and fast moving. Those are the times when you really are... feeling bright.

In energy field healing, a key objective is to clear the energy field of emotional and mental 'debris'. Using specialised techniques, we can clear away the heavier and more dense energy forms that are restricting the flow of fresh, light energy flowing through the system. I have literally seen clients come into the clinic room miserable, hopeless and struggling, and leave an hour later with a spring in their step, bright, positive and looking forward to taking charge of the things they want to change in their lives. It really has been, as simple as that - the application of the will and skill of the healer to clear and transform the pre-existing non-serving energies that are incapacitating the client.

Tips on developing your energy awareness of feelings:-

1. Allow yourself the good grace to feel what you are feeling in any given moment, such that you do not let your mind instantly take over, analyse the feeling, and dismiss or limit its relevance.

2. Accept that it is human and okay, to feel the full range of feelings that you encounter. It is your actual response to any given situation that will ultimately make the difference to outcomes and circumstances.

3. Understand that others' feelings will be directed towards you. That's a function of the energetic relationship we have with each other. You do not have to own or absorb another's feelings, you can make an alternate choice.

4. Recognise those times when you are emotionally impacted, such that you cannot identify the nature of your true feeling. Withdraw from any such scenario until you feel stable and aware.

5. Accept and acknowledge that you are already carrying a multitude of emotional resonances from the past and that these need your focus and attention to clear and release. This is the process of self-healing and the clearer you become, the more capacity for life you will manage.

6. If you are experiencing powerful emotions that you feel you cannot deal with alone, then seek support and assistance. Carrying emotions that overwhelm you is a disempowered state. Healing, therapy or the support of a professional psychologist is a solution and will aid you.

7. Realise that when you are in a distressed emotional state, you will react to circumstances or situations. In a reactive state, you are not in command of the energetic flow. In such scenarios, you may speak or act in a manner not in accord with your true nature or your desired intent. Remove yourself from the scenario until you are calm and stable.

My recommendation to you would be to become as emotionally clear as possible by healing and releasing any past wounds and traumas. This is so vital, because of one simple truth - the energy forms resonating within your field are radiating out their essence and will attract more of the same.

I previously mentioned that in energy like-attracts-like. Your energy - who you are as an energetic being - is you as a consciousness. We reside within a unified field of consciousness, of which you are commanding a small aspect by way of your individual presence upon the physical Earth. Consciousness will always seek to enhance and to be in a state of wholeness. The manner by which it seeks to maintain its own unification, is by way of resonance. Consciousness aligns with matching resonance. Hence, in energy, like-attracts-like. Similar resonance comes together to be whole. It is the means by which we attract people, opportunities, potentials, occurrences and happenings into our lives.

Therefore, if your field is holding a mass of conflicting and erupting emotional and mental energy forms, they will naturally attract more of the same. All life experience has to be acknowledged, understood, learned from and released. Your subtle emotional and mental intelligence is always seeking to experience, enhance and then move on. I would ask you to take responsibility for your energetic state and make a commitment to help yourself become clear.

"I live a very busy life and have learnt how to manage it more effectively. I recognise when I am getting stressed, overwhelmed, being over-emotional, or over-thinking and have learnt energy techniques to help identify and minimise such overload by cleansing, healing, balancing and protecting my energies. As a result, I make much more fruitful decisions in my life and have an increased flow of synchronicity and intuition.

I work freelance in an array of different environments including offices, festivals/events, TV studios and film sets. Often these environments are emotionally highly charged and can be very draining. I have developed my skills to help maintain my energy levels in a more positive way so that I am less affected by negative situations, people and environments.

I feel energy awareness has helped me understand my own experiences and come to greater comprehension about life and the universe in which we live. As a result I feel much more connected to and aware of the world: to people, earth, animals, spirit, the universe, and my place within that. I couldn't have such faith without experiencing this for myself and without the knowledge I have gained through energy awareness."

E Jeng, Actress, Creative Artist &
Advanced Level Energy Field Healer

Let's Go Mental | 5

"Your mind is a powerful thing, capable of creating and conducting your life, but it functions as a product of the feelings you experience."

The energies of your mental processing - thoughts, ideas, intents, and so on, move through your energy field in a very different way to feelings. They are held in forms of electrical impulses and patterns which circulate through layers of electrical activity. I call these 'mental layers'. These electrical energy charges move through the field within fine filigree-like lines of connectivity. It looks like a grid or framework of light when the mental layers are strong and intact.

Try to see that as continuously flowing energy activity and every time you have a thought, an additional charge of energy moves through these grid-like layers. Every time someone sends you any mental energy transaction – a thought, a communication, a question – anything that requires you to think... then imagine even more charge of energy travelling through that grid.

The mind is a powerful thing, capable of creating and conducting your life, and also of managing your health and well-being. Much has already been written on the subject of the power of the mind on your health and outlook, so what I would like to address is the nature of your thoughts, how they reside within the energy, and how you apply them in life.

As previously stated, you feel first. The thought process is then a product of the nature and essence of the feeling experienced. That is why it is so important to know what you are feeling, because without recognising the feeling, you cannot understand your thinking. Think about times you have encountered when you cannot work out the meaning of a situation or indeed, how it got to the way it was. Thoughts will just loop over and over in your mind, as you try to make sense of things. Also, the occasions when a problem is mentally tormenting you and you seemingly cannot find the answers.

Those times occur when you have not identified the initiating feeling, or understood how the feelings of a situation are impacting you. The truth is, once we identify the feelings involved, the solutions and possible outcomes become obvious. Truly, one of the most potent things you can ever ask yourself about a situation is "how do I feel about this?".

When your emotions are clear, it provides the necessary space for your thoughts to flow correctly in sequence and for ideas and processes to function unhindered. Together, the emotional and mental functions create your reality. Your ability to be aware is dependent on both those aspects being strong and clear. A balanced way of living, therefore, is to have both feeling and thought incorporated fully in your daily life process, whereby you recognise and validate what you are truly feeling in order to successfully apply the mindful process.

The most vital thing to understand is that as the electrical pulses of mental processing pass through the layers, they can trigger the potency of any emotional energy forms residing there. Your thinking might then become inflamed or elaborated by the nature and energy charge of that emotional 'debris'.

A simple example of that might be... someone at work says something which upsets you. Shortly after, you find yourself thinking through what they've said and getting more annoyed over it. Then suddenly, your mind connects back to a time someone else said something similar. In no time at all, you start to think about all the times that 'type' of thing has been said to you. Then emotions start to flare up within you based on those random thoughts and the whole situation becomes completely out of proportion. Recognise that? It's what I call a 'cascading trigger'. A thought pattern connects to a dormant emotional 'form' and starts a 'domino' effect, until the situation becomes completely changed from its original form. Without being aware of the emotional content of your field, or the effects of how subtle energies connect different aspects of you through the field, you would not be able to identify how these complex transactions are affecting your thinking.

Your own inner desires are the most powerful point from which your thought processes can originate. Your creative abilities depend on that inner impulse to drive your desires into manifest reality. In a state of good self-awareness, you can be true to your inner desires and apply your intelligence to progress, create and achieve in life.

Reacting rather than creating

What is more common though, is the thought process being a reactive consequence rather than a creative intent. This happens for the majority of people, for most of the time. It is just a default mode of unawareness. Reactivity predominantly occurs when there are pre-existing, unacknowledged feelings in your energy system. The presence of those emotional energy forms and patterns, hinders the clarity of the mental processing. They behave like a field of 'debris' and 'contamination' through which all your thinking and calculating has to pass. If you come to understand that thinking is a product of how you feel or have felt, then you can appreciate that there will be times when you think, act and react, outside of reason or sense. The times when you exasperate yourself with your own deeds and end up saying "I don't know what I was thinking!" or, "I don't know what came over me!".

To have clarity with 'thinking for yourself', you have to first identify the feelings that are active within you. Your thought process will be driven and influenced by these feelings, so if you ignore or invalidate them, you are blinding yourself to the real motivations of your thinking. Since your thoughts are most likely to lead to action, it is vital that you understand the true motivation.

The 'reactive' state also occurs when you have unknowingly colluded with another's thoughts. Those are the times when you just don't 'think for yourself'. Many people live in a reactionary state, simply aligning themselves to the thoughts, actions and creations of others. Often the outcome of such collusions is an array of life dramas and challenging situations that create disappointment and confusion.

Herein lay the key to the production of dramas, of life circumstances and situations which are difficult, incomprehensible and not desired. Life's drama, preventable happenings and unwanted outcomes, are all products of people not knowing or directing their true intentions. Without awareness of the true intentions, you cannot direct or command your life in a purposeful or meaningful way.

On those occasions when you are not 'thinking for yourself', you may be merely regurgitating the thoughts and intentions of others. Each person has their own motivations and driving feelings and ultimately they may not be truly in accord with your own. This is reactive living, rather than creative living. If you regularly find yourself saying things like... "I don't know what happened, how did it turn out like that?" or "I wish I'd never got involved with them in the first place," or "I can't believe it ended up like that", then you are reactive living.

Personal responsibility for your own creations

When you are not aware of your own motivating feelings, then you are thinking without clarity or authenticity. Your actions and outcomes will most likely mislead you. The consequences and outcomes of your actions will ensue, become an active part of your life and then deliver to you your daily happenings.

If you are continuously living through circumstances not of your choosing, then you need to explore the original motivations that went into creating them.

Within truly creative energy flows, you are responsible for all you create. It is worth asking yourself, did you create true to your inner being? Personal responsibility is a fascinating thing. You would be able to look back now - and you won't have to go far - and bring to mind a life situation that you got into by reacting to someone else's intentions and/or actions. And you'll look back and scold yourself for not "seeing it coming", or for not stopping matters before they "went too far". Are you recognising that?

In energy terms, in consciousness, we are all creators. Big or small, we create constantly as we go through each day. The person who originates a creation, holds its intent. That intent is then transmitted out to the people it needs to involve. Within the subtle energy flows an energy dynamic may be created. At that point, others join the energy flow and 'take on board' the nature of the intent. They will alter its flow in some way, because they have added their own personal energy to the 'flow of intent', but ultimately, the responsibility for the idea/project/creation lay with the originator.

Now, consider for a few moments, are you mainly an originator? Or are you one who colludes? Do you create from your own ideas and motivations? Or do you most often join collaboration with others or just follow the crowd, and then maybe get disappointed with the outcomes?

Whether you realise it or not, you participate in many different energy dynamics. They exist at home with your family members, within your social circle of friends, and the most fragile one of all, at work in your employment.

If you view life events through 'energy eyes' the whole process of creation takes on a different perspective. You can see your own role and participation in things, and with growing awareness, you soon come to understand how you are the creator, or not, of your own life. By understanding the energy flows, you can choose and decide for yourself which aspects you would like to change, initiate or conclude.

If you are mainly an originator, then you are likely living an empowered life. You are 'making things happen' and pursuing your choices. You then only need to ask what feelings are motivating the origination of your creations?

- Why are you choosing to do what you do?
- Who is it serving?
- Who benefits?
- Who loses?
- What contribution are you making to the greater whole?

The world is full of powerful people, creating every day from motivations that do not serve well! You would not need to look far to see someone who is corrupting or abusing the power or authority entrusted to them. I hope your first choice would be to enrich the lives of others and of yourself. That assurance comes from understanding your true inner motivations, the feelings that drive your desires.

Be true to yourself and fully understand your motivations before you put energy into action. Remember, you are responsible for the flow of your creations and how they impact the lives of others.

Collaborations bind your energies to the command of another

Let's take a deeper look at collaboration - those times when you go along with the plans and ideas of others. When you join in with someone's idea/creative intent you join their energy dynamic, and align to it your own energy resources.

On a subtle energy level, this is the equivalent of endorsement. Energetically, you put your personal power into the continuation of the flow of the idea/ creative intent being originated by another. It is wise, therefore, to ask yourself right at the beginning... why? Do you truly agree with this idea? Is it in accord with your core values? Does the concept of this creation make you feel good? Will it serve well? Who will benefit? Is it a worthy contribution? Do you truly choose to align your inner power and energy resources with this person's intention and creative flow?

Those questions need to be asked right at the beginning if you are to prevent future frustration, stress, resentment, conflict or personal devaluation. If you spend multiple hours of your day enacting a process which you neither emotionally support nor believe in, you need to reflect upon why.

Unhappiness with choices - in a job, relationship, or at home - is a primary cause of stress and stress related illness. On a subtle energy level, you may now perhaps see why. If you carry on regardless, the energy forms will flow through you in conflict. Such emotional and mental conflict will hinder all aspects of your energy system, creating density, stagnation and distress.

To an energy field healer scanning through the field, mental stress within the system feels like masses of colliding particles hitting the hand. These are literally charged particles bouncing around in the energy field, colliding with each other. They are distressed particles. Stress consumes the resources within the energy system, such that the physical body no longer gets the fuel it needs. Fatigue, aches, muscle tension and lowered immunity are the first obvious signs of low energy fuel.

Once the energy system begins to run on low fuel, the energetic processing will start to malfunction. One of the first things to deteriorate is mental processing, reasoning, memory and correct analysis. As the energy system tries to readdress the lack of fuel to the mental functioning, it takes energy from the primary system - the emotions.

Once energy resource is diverted away from the emotional elements, the energetic ‘debris’ that resides in the field is no longer contained or positioned and you are no longer in emotional control. So those old feelings and patterns get ‘fired up’, start bouncing around and you become emotionally volatile. You will very soon start to feel overwhelmed. You will most certainly feel distressed by the instability of the energies ‘bouncing’ around your system.

Should the stress situation continue, the resulting imbalance and breakdown of the subtle energy system becomes inevitable. The sheer pressure of the unstable energies will impact. Such a person is no longer making sense. Such a person becomes irrational, they will be heading out of control. Such a person is no longer in command of their life.

Whenever you feel discontent or find yourself ‘hating’ something, dreading its arrival, or feeling deep contempt whenever you have to be in it, you should stop and assess your choices. You are worth more than to do this to yourself. These aspects are energy environments, energy forms and influences. You are not exempt from their effects, because you are in that energetic state. It may not be clear at the time how you got into such a situation, but you can certainly consider how to remove yourself from it in a supportive and kind manner.

If you are involved in something that you feel is a chore, then it is obvious your passion is not in it. If any aspect of your life does not enrich or nourish you, then it is most likely not in accord with your inner feelings and desires. If you continue, that ‘something’ will consume you energetically and create its own difficulties and hindrance. It will undoubtedly affect your peace of mind, it will stir non-serving emotions and it will prompt you to act out of alignment with your core values and true desires.

If you have colluded in any creation, then you remain energetically partly responsible. If an outcome is destructive, if it hurts others, if it becomes non-virtuous, you are not innocent in the process. Not being the originator does not release you from some of the responsibility of the outcomes. If you have colluded with the creation and added your personal power to it, you will inevitably live through some of the drama or difficulty it creates. That is why it is so vital to assess your life activity at commencement, before you jump on board with any collaborative situations. Know your own true motivations, so that you can be answerable for your actions when you have to make your own personal assessment on the quality of your life.

Within the flow of your energy, you are a constantly flowing mass of complex and evolving mental debris or intent. Everything has to be processed, acknowledged, understood, responded to, learned from, expanded upon or dismissed. You are a very busy human being. Mental energies need to be in constant management through the application of higher intelligence. Higher intelligence is a high frequency activity, it relies upon the core primary power of good feelings in order to formulate a correct life process. So never dismiss the inner responsibilities of understanding your own feelings - they are primary to the creation of all aspects of your life and the powerful driver of your mindful intent.

"I felt like I was looking for something. I didn't know what that something was, I was searching. I went to Church, I trained in reflexology, then Reiki, but nothing seemed to satisfy me. Someone recommended Sue Zange and her training and development courses. This was 2001. I loved the atmosphere and Sue kept us enthralled in her subject. Sue has developed unique training programmes for raising awareness.

I couldn't tell you back then what my soul was craving for. I now know it was the awakening of my spiritual self, and the calling of my physical body to make change.

I never thought then, that I would be talking about subtle energies or raising your vibration, but that is what I do now on a daily basis. The techniques help you make changes that will enhance your life, so you can go about your daily 'doings' feeling grounded and secure.

Energy awareness is a way of life, and brings light in to the darkest of days. But you have to live it, to know it. To look within is the journey of the soul to fulfilment."

L. Cooke, Operating Theatre Assistant
& Certified Inspirit Teacher

Viewing Through Energy Eyes | 6

"Seeing life through an alternate perspective offers you options to change and improve life beyond measure."

At any given point of your waking day, you are receiving emotional and mental transmissions from others. Personal interactions, phone calls, conversations, communications... all providing raw energetic data that is flowing into your personal energy field. Both the emotional content and the mental intent of those interactions, is arriving in your energetic space.

You will be listening, absorbing, formulating, contemplating, investigating, concluding or acting, in response to the transmissions received from others. Whether you have realised it or not, these transmissions will be activating or generating an emotional response within you, because everything that happens to you, all experience, is designed to engage with you on that primary level of feeling.

In addition to all that you receive, you are energetically transmitting out your thoughts, feelings, intentions, ideas, creative flows and so on, to others. You are continuously energetically busy in your daily life activities. I refer to these transmissions and receipts as energy transactions.

So imagine your field as an ongoing process factory, dealing with the incoming and outgoing transactions, and actively working towards an outcome of creative and valuable expression in life.

Each and every day you will process masses of energy transactions, but depending on how busy you are, you will also have some transactions left unprocessed. The unfulfilled or uncleared residues of each day's activity will remain in your field. These forms will join with all the pre-existing emotional and mental energies already in your field from previous activities and experiences. These include feelings you have never dealt with, all the emotional 'baggage' you carry, everything you have never been able to forgive, release, or let go of. It all becomes compounded with your own vague thoughts, snippets of others' thoughts and ideas, bits of conversation, the words, the sounds, every thread of energy data that you have not fully processed. I refer to unprocessed forms of energy data as 'energy debris'.

If you've ever wondered why you got so very upset over something minor or trivial, it's because the energy of that situation joined with pre-existing patterns and grew larger and more impacting. You would have no understanding of that without subtle energy awareness, because seeing life through 'energy eyes' offers a different perspective. It is a unique and empowering way of viewing all of life's activities and experiences. It is an insight that offers you a broader understanding of everything you are involved in.

If you come to understand that the majority of life processing and activity is taking place unknown to you, on the invisible subtle energetic level, then the real issue is how to discover what is really going on. How do you discover the degree of influence and the key driving factors which are currently outside your understanding? This book is about helping you discover that.

The processing of which you are mentally and emotionally aware in your conscious mind, is only a fraction of what is actually occurring. There are multiple layers of complex functioning taking place, of which you are currently consciously unaware. It's an invisible world. Until you purposely direct your attention towards it, the activity will remain unknown to you.

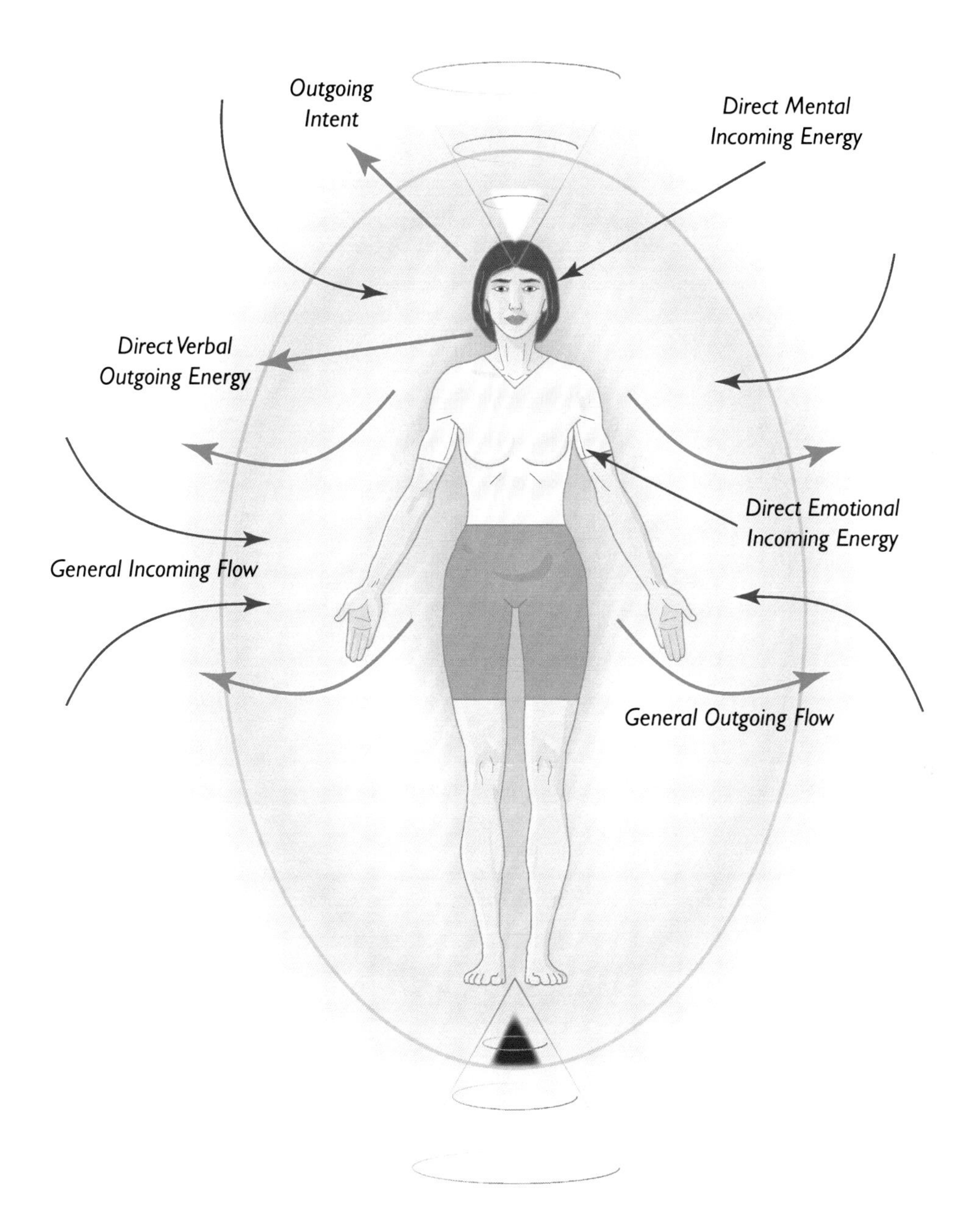

Picture 6 - Incoming and Outgoing Energy Transactions

Do not extend beyond your energy capacity

Everyone has a limit to their energetic capacity, the point at which the system becomes full of subtle data, processing and receipts on an energetic level. Put simply, the amount of activity you can 'hold' at any given time. A strong energy system has a greater capacity than a weak energy system. Strong and balanced energy will flow faster than weak energy. As such, strong energy will process subtle data more rapidly, it can apply higher intelligence more easily. As a result, a person with strong energy can be busier, get more things done, achieve more in allotted time, due to their ability to process more efficiently.

When an energy transaction occurs for someone of strong energy presence, it moves speedily through the emotional and mental processing and initiates a balanced response. That energy flow then concludes, or initiates further outward action by being processed and redirected towards its next purpose. Space is then made in the energy system for the next transaction to flow in. Strong energy equals greater capacity.

Throughout my working life I have had people comment on how much I can get done. I have always been extremely efficient and productive. I could do as much work in three hours as the majority of others would take a whole day to achieve. I didn't realise, until I came to understand subtle energy, that this is due to energy capacity. I know now that the strength, clarity and balance of my energy field is what dictates my progression through each working day.

What is important to know and understand, is what happens if you reach your capacity but still continue your busy-ness. In such a situation your energy will overload. It will literally become over-full of more energy transactions than you have the ability to deal with.

In energy terms, that's an over-burdened state and you actually do not have the capacity to energetically process and manage everything that you're involved with. The energy then starts to speed up in an attempt to process quicker. Those are the times when we feel 'het-up', fraught, rushing, anxious about carrying on and getting things done.

If you have exceeded your energetic capacity, you are beyond the bounds by which you can command your life process and content. Many energy forms within the field may then become unmanageable and chaotic. A chaotic state in the energy is when the transactions are bouncing around randomly, because they are no longer under your command. They've 'gone rogue'. That's what chaos is - energies which are not flowing by command.

There's one major aspect of chaotic energy of which you should be aware... it sparks off events and random happenings. So, accidents happen, things get broken, arguments flare up, drama heightens, the unexpected occurs, sudden things happen. It's an uncontrolled state, and it will play itself out, if you do not regain command. That's why it is so important to prevent a chaotic state.

You may want to stop for a moment here and consider how often your life is out of command - when it is chaotic, stressful or overwhelming. Now try to see that as an energetic state.

Imagine the times you have become so over-busy that you lose focus on some of the situations and events that are occurring. The energetic forms of those aspects upon which you lose focus become chaotic and the undirected energies have to find somewhere to go. In this state, you become at the mercy of the pre-existing energies playing themselves out, until the energy momentum is exhausted. You are then left with a set of circumstances that need your attention in a different way - usually, damage control.

Once you move beyond your ability to command your life on the subtle energetic level, conflicts arise in the energy through the chaotic process. The consequence is stress, because you can no longer give all your activity your focus and attention. With the energies no longer within your command, the simple law of cause and effect will rampage its way through your day.

The nature of energy is like-attracts-like. So chaotic energy forms will combine with other similar energy patterns within your field and start attracting more of the same. Trouble makes trouble. Stress makes stress.

The confusion of chaos - the pressure of stress

Chaotic energies will create a scenario where you are confused and unclear. You may misunderstand incoming communications, be unable to recall information clearly, and story lines can become mixed up. Chaos takes the energy flows out of natural sequence and therefore memory recall is one of the first casualties of this state. As it continues you will be feeling overwhelmed and overloaded, disorganised and 'fed up' (you have been fed too much incoming data!).

At this stage, if you could see the energy as I do, you would discover randomly moving, dull grey swirls of suppressed emotions and ideas. Within that dense swirling of greyness, sparks of electrical activity will be discharging as the mental processing tries to re-ignite and reactivate flow and sequence. Lines of energy intent will try to move outwards awkwardly, but then may thrust themselves back into the system because they are undirected and lack clear intention. A sea of outward and inward energy motions rocking the field back and forth.

From my experience as an energy field healer, the most common occurrence of chaotic energy is with working mums. Many of them are juggling so many different aspects of life, all of which are important - home, children, spouse, career - that their energy fields are ripe for overloading. I have also seen it in high level executives and directors, who try to manage more people, projects and responsibilities than they have capacity for. These clients comment that they feel renewed and rebuilt after their healing session, and that's actually what has occurred. The energy field has been cleared of the debris and chaotic forms, re-stabilised and re-energised with new fresh flows of source energy.

I would ask you to consider the broader picture of energies 'out of command'. All of us, as human beings, are responsible for important things. We make decisions and take actions that will affect the lives of others, in small ways, in big ways. In the case of the mother - she needs to guide her children towards intelligent and moral living. The executive is driving a business that upholds the livelihoods of others.

Do we not owe a responsibility to each other to tend, affect and share with each other in as clear, directive and compassionate a way as possible? Chaos negates that.

A continuation of a chaotic state creates its own failures in daily life processing. The inevitable consequence is stress. In the subtle energy system, stress is conflict. It occurs when two opposing forces of energy come together, creating pressure in the system. Such pressure blocks the natural flows, dulls intelligent processing and oppresses the forthcoming of feelings within the system.

A chaotic state results in stress due to the will, intent and emotional drive being unable to correct the situation. We feed our will-power into the state, trying to resolve and restore some sort of balance and acceptability, to put things right. However, the random nature of the chaotic elements will just keep opposing the will, and hence pressure is created. These are the times when 'your head's all over the place' and you cannot think straight; when you're feeling het-up and distraught and don't know why; and when you want everything to stop and go away, because you can't cope.

As well as chaos due to over-busyness, there is another major cause of stress in the energy system, and that's to do with your own values, morals and desire for good living. Within you, is held your own moral code of what you believe is right, fair, just and acceptable. Your inner core values, your moral righteousness, are an aspect of your consciousness, and when your energy is clear, you will always apply those principles of consciousness to your own rightful daily living.

If free to do so, you will make choices in life that are fully in accord with your inner moral code and values. However, it doesn't always come to pass that life presents circumstances within which we can always make such higher choices. If you are doing something that actually you don't want to do, don't agree with, or don't believe in, then such action will create an opposing force to your inner will/desires/beliefs/value code. For example, if you are going out to work each day to a place you dislike and don't want to be, and working with people you don't 'fit in' with, then your action is a direct conflict with your desires and feelings. Or maybe you are in a relationship that is not of a mutually shared and loving nature, perhaps with someone you don't truly desire to be with. Perhaps you have to comply to societal or institutional rules or policies that do not adhere to your own views of 'the right way to do things'. These are simple examples of a state of opposing forces.

Wherever or however your actions and deeds do not correspond fully with your inner moral code and standards, an opposing force will exist in the energy system. Such conflict will restrict the natural flows of emotion, intent and creativity in your every day life activities.

It doesn't just go away because you think it has

Remember, emotional stress is created by opposing energy forces - that's two energy resonances (vibrations) colliding in your system creating a discordance that potentially can break down the cohesive flow of your entire energy structure. A state of stress is a threat to your well-being and we have base programming that activates the moment any threat arrives. Immediately, the mind will pursue a coping mechanism, based on functions or behaviours it has previously learned, in order to try to calm some of the energetic stress. One of the primary coping mechanisms we have is re-positioning.

Re-positioning, on a physical level, might enact as you changing your itinerary or commitments, delegating to others, re-managing the priorities and putting aside some tasks. Maybe that re-positioning is emotional or mental, such as the times we say "Oh, it doesn't matter, forget about it" and we brush it aside. Or we might say "It's silly, I shouldn't let these things get to me" and then we move on to the next task. That may often be how we get on with the day.

However, in the energy, it looks very different. Re-positioning in the subtle energy means you will move and relocate certain energy forms to elsewhere within your field so that they are out of your immediate conscious awareness. You may think you are managing things and coping, but what you are actually doing, is just delaying the inevitable.

Let me conjure an example for you here... imagine you have boxed up a lot of your home 'junk' and are going to store it in a spare room. These are things you can't yet throw out, or give to charity, because you haven't yet sorted through them. By putting your boxes into the spare room, you've made a little more space in your living area. After some time, you find you have a few more boxes of 'junk'. Then a few more. So you continue to fill up the spare room. At some point, you're going to have to re-organise that room, because the piling up of boxes will become unmanageable. So, you re-position the boxes in the spare room, which may then give you a little more space to add even more boxes. Eventually, the room space could become entirely full of boxes filled with stuff you have never sorted and there is now so much of it, that it would be overwhelming to confront it and clear it. So it gets left.

That is the equivalent of what can occur in your energy field if you re-position the life aspects that you do not have the time, energy or motivation to deal with. It builds up until the power and density of it tips the balance and creates a catastrophic breakdown in your energy system. Those are the times when you become physically ill, mentally ill or exhausted, or emotionally distraught and unstable. Having taken your energy over capacity, the stress and re-positioning has left multiple aspects unattended, and a crisis situation will strike at you.

From my years of clinic experience, you would be stunned to know the percentage of people who live in this manner - reposition rather than clear out or opt out. You would also be amazed to know how many people know they are stressed, doing too much and on overload, and continue to do the same living pattern day after day. The longer you continue to 're-position' as a coping strategy, the bigger the future problem you are creating. In the subtle energy system, as you build up the re-positioned energy forms, they start to combine and ultimately create an effect that is similar to building a wall around you or barricading yourself in. The effect is numbness, you stop feeling, stop thinking, lose inspiration, lose the desire to move forwards. It's a stagnant state.

Every aspect you reposition, will ultimately have to come to your attention again. All things are created through energy form, they have momentum, an intention, and a time line through which they are flowing. When you re-position something, the energy remains active and therefore, will have to come to your attention again at whatever moment it can, in whatever way it can, in order to be dealt with. In the meantime, it will always be lingering in the background, resonating and attracting more of the same. All you have done is delayed the inevitable.

This is an unacceptable lifestyle, it is energetically imbalanced. It does not serve you well, it is dis-empowering and ultimately, it will become completely unmanageable. So can I ask you now to take a few minutes to think about your coping methods when you get busy. Look at this through 'energy eyes', it will offer you a different perspective, a higher perspective.

Can't re-position? Then you might blast it out towards others!

Another overload coping mechanism is expulsion! Those are the occasions of outburst, temper tantrums, ranting, explosions of uncontrolled behaviour. In such occurrences, you are trying to expel the overload and pressure that is within your energy. The sheer frustration of feeling compressed by the overload, vents itself, usually towards whoever is in the 'firing line' at the time. Something, or someone, has triggered the final collapse of any intelligent command in your system and that tension and overload will start bursting into the World.

I know you have experienced that scenario, we all have. But you will not have known why. The explosion occurs and then you have to repair the damage it has caused, if you can. Later, upon reflection, you feel the remorse, sorrow, or guilt and you can't work out how you got to that state and why your behaviour deteriorated below your own values standard.

Without deeper insight, without subtle energy awareness, you may never know how or why that came about. The consequences of such explosions change life circumstances, sometimes they can change the course of destinies. Internally, you will attempt to change that behaviour - trying to correct something of which you do not understand the structure, nature or purpose.

Real breakthroughs in changes of behaviour come when we comprehend the influences and motivational factors behind them. That exists in the fine and invisible subtle energy infrastructure of your life.

Even a little awareness of those contributing subtle energy factors will help you to make better choices, more serving decisions, engage more fully with your feelings and most especially, behave differently. Discovering why something has occurred helps us to grow, to change, to become greater than a set of circumstances dictates to us.

Once you accept that energy forms, patterns and transactions are a major part of your daily activity, you can engage in awareness of how it may be affecting you. Most especially, you can take time out to tend your energy system, keep yourself clear and balance your life activity more well.

It is obvious though that continuous daily living at over-capacity is unwise. This scenario creates the perfect recipe for ill-health. And that's the real issue. Continuing with a lifestyle which overloads you energetically will lead to a natural consequence and usually, that is ill-health - physical, mental or emotional.

If you were to pay attention for just one day and view your world through energy eyes, what would you see. How many transactions come your way and what are their resonance? If you can see everything as energy - the mind, the emotions, consciousness - then everything becomes manageable. All life activity is able to be within your creative command and intent - from the most minor matters you deal with, up to the most major of crises. Your life looks different when it is viewed from an energy perspective. I'd like to share Nicki's story with you, because she applied her energy understanding to completely restore and regenerate her life.

Hear Nicki's Story:

"In 2006 I felt empty, disillusioned, stressed and 'burnt out'. Working full time, usually fourteen hour days in a very demanding environment, caring for a young child and trying to keep all the balls in the air was difficult to say the least. As a single parent, I was struggling with the many demands that everyday life was throwing at me.

I recognised that I was mentally and physically exhausted and in need of respite on both counts. One evening, I found Sue's website and read about Subtle Energies and her abilities. I signed up for one of Sue's weekend courses and wasn't entirely sure what it would entail. To say that Sue's courses are unique would be an understatement. The whole weekend was filled with wonderment and awe. I experienced calmness and hope in equal measure.

This was the start of my own personal development and growth. Since 2006 it's been my pleasure to attend more of these unique courses and study days, every single one has been an exceptional experience, providing inspirational information that resonates deep within the soul. So much so, that I decided to train in Energy Field Healing.

Subtle Energy awareness has given me the confidence to leave my full time job and follow my heart by starting my own business. The skills are all encompassing, enriching and enhance all aspects of my life. By utilising and employing the various skills and knowledge I have been taught, my relationships, both personally and professionally have benefitted immensely. My clients and patients have found Energy Field Healing a wonderful, individual experience, unlike any other healing modality.

On a personal level, I feel happier, calmer and very grateful that I found Sue Zange and Subtle Energy Awareness. Thankfully, I'm no longer the person I was in 2006! We all need this knowledge in our lives."

Nicki Jenkins, Advanced Energy Field Healer,
& Hypnotherapist Dip.Hyp.CS

Nicki is a wonderful example of how, with just a little more insight into life, we can all make better choices and decisions about the way we live. Her full time job was impacting both her lifestyle and her well-being. When she was able to see the nature of her life through subtle energy awareness, it gave her the strength and conviction to make the changes needed to improve both her daily life and her longer term creative potentials.

"Since training in subtle energy awareness I have found that life has opened up for me on a whole new level. I see potentials and value in areas that before would not have even been in my awareness.

I understand now the interactions and transactions that take place in the energy and this helps me to manage situations differently. We are often wanting to break free and make a change to live a better more fulfilling life, but something holds us back, an invisible force and we are unable to find the answer. Usually we give up, resign ourselves to 'this is my lot in life' and plod on.

It doesn't have to be like that. By understanding how the energy works and the dynamics we are involved in, we can achieve whatever we set our minds to. It is the key to finding your own empowerment in life. Once you become energy aware there is no going back. Most likely for the first time in your life you will be truly in command of your own destiny and could any of us want more than that? To be able to have the skill set to achieve whatever we set our minds to and to have the trust and faith to know the conclusion will be one of completion."

S Tranter, Business Proprietor &
Advanced Level Energy Field Healer

Energy Skills to Manage Life | 7

"Apply some simple skills to transform the essence and vibration of your energy... your presence. Then you will be living your light."

You can only truly be empowered from the moment you choose to be in command of your own life. From the moment you acknowledge that you are responsible for your own life, your own creations, and your own responses.

An empowered life is that of a creator, an originator of ideas, someone who is aware of the feelings that drive those ideas.

So, time to assess the content of your life:

1. How many aspects of your daily life activities are your own true creations, originating from within your own creative thought process?

2. Of those creations, can you identify the feelings that brought them into form? Do you recognise and understand your inner motivation?

3. How many aspects of your daily life are in response to or reacting to, the needs, demands, wants, instructions or expectations of others?

4. Of those aspects you collude in, do you know the true motivations of the originator and do you agree with and align to, those motivations?

Take the time you need to consider these four points right now. What you discover may surprise you. Remember what we're talking about here - all your life transactions are aspects in which you have invested your energy. They are either enriching you or consuming you. It's time to take account of the situation.

Those aspects that are enriching you will be generating joy, fun and pleasure. Whenever you are engaged with things you like to do, enjoy, or love, your energy naturally expands and becomes a self-generating entity. You will literally be re-sourcing yourself and your energy will remain buoyant and light, and will be flowing at a high frequency. You will feel good about doing such activities and will gain enrichment.

Those activities you do not enjoy are consuming the energy system, they will fatigue and bore you. You may feel resentment at having to do them. You will evade or avoid them whenever possible and may actually use more energy resources to achieve such avoidance than to actually do them! Such activity may make you feel dull and despondent, because it is draining your energy resources and lowering the vibration within the field. These activities will lessen and devalue you - emotionally, mentally and spiritually.

Your first course of action, wherever possible, should be to withdraw from all creations, intentions and collusions for which you do not feel true, joyful motivation. That will include those which are not in accord with your values. I fully appreciate that withdrawal from these activities may take a little time. You may have to replan and rethink the strategy for your life. You also need to understand your responsibilities to others for all that you have been involved with. So do consider carefully the effect that your corrective choices will have on others and deal with it kindly, compassionately and considerately.

That clearing action will likely release a good 40% of the non-serving activities out of your energy system. When you contemplate the nature of your activities, you may be surprised to discover just how much you are involved with, which you really would prefer not to be. When we make choices without awareness, we may become involved in things and discover our unhappiness with the choice a little way into it, but then feel obligated to continue. You may also realise what you are not involved with, which you would like to be.

You then need to make your life-stress analysis. You need to start to really take notice when you are beginning to feel stressed and overloaded as you experience each day/week/month. This is a simple development in raising your own self-awareness. Bring on board a new rule for you - when such stresses arise, STOP. You need to retreat from or lessen, the life activities which you know will consume and damage your energy system. In a state of stress, the only rightful course of action is to stop the inflow of energetic data, thereby giving your energy time to clear, release and re-balance.

There is a reason that spiritual practices such as meditation and yoga are growing ever more popular. They are an ideal way in which to stop the busy activity of your life. When I train my students in energy life-management skills, I encourage them to take 10 minutes away from all activity and action three or four times a day. In those 10 minutes, they just stop and focus on being still, allowing the processing of the mind to clear its backlog and become quiet. They learn how to discharge the energetic debris from their field by command. They return to feeling centred, focused and ready to continue.

There are some very simple energy techniques that will help you manage your energy flows. The first I will introduce is the 'Disconnection Command'. It is a way to command the excess energy forms and debris out of your field. Please always remember that energy follows thought. So by applying a command, the energy will move in accord. It's a simple, yet very effective technique. You can use this command whenever you are beginning to feel stressed, hectic, or overloaded with activity.

The 'Disconnection Command'

"I DISCONNECT AND DISENGAGE FROM ALL ENERGIES THAT ARE NOT SERVING MY HIGHEST PURPOSE AT THIS TIME. I DISCONNECT NOW."

This is a statement of command, and the energy will follow your intent. Say it with conviction and your energy field will naturally release out a great deal of the energy connections and debris which are not serving you well.

Too much involvement in the lives of others

The next recommended course of action is to focus your awareness on how much you are involved in other people's lives. Are you regularly involved in all their happenings and dramas? Do you have friends who get on the phone to tell you everything that is occurring in their lives? Are you the one to whom everyone runs to off-load their woes and worries?

See that through 'energy eyes' now. For everything you are engaged with, you are inviting in the energy form and imprint. You are 'filling up' your energy field with the life activities of others. More powerfully, you are joining their energy dynamics, and that may consume your resources.

The energy forms of all that others involve you with, will attach themselves (like-for-like) to any feelings and thoughts already in your field, which are of a similar resonance. So, your existing feelings and thoughts will expand and become more overly important or imposing, and you may not realise why. Nor will you understand the consequences of these subtle energy transactions. If in conversation with another, you find yourself saying things like "That happened to me..." and then you start conveying your own story, I can guarantee you have just activated your own dormant energetic patterns. The two of you will join in a dynamic of energy exchange, during which you will be influencing each other, and changing the nature of the energy forms. You might recognise this as someone else 'charging you up', or adding 'fuel to the fire'.

Once you are exchanging energies in this way, the dynamic expands, becomes more active and starts to engage your resources. You will be absorbing influence and intent from whoever is involved, together with the emotional and mental content they are projecting. How did a small issue suddenly become so large? Well, you grew it in your energy field!

I am not suggesting to you that all conversations and interactions with others will always energetically consume or aggravate you. I am asking you to recognise what occurs when you are unaware of your own issues and therefore have no command over what activates within your energy. I am also asking that you recognise when you are willingly becoming involved in others' dramas and issues.

There is one major element to subtle energy knowledge of which you have to become aware at this stage. When you absorb the energetic thoughts and feelings of others, you have no command of them. You did not originate them and therefore, you cannot command their flow or intent. You will have absorbed an energy form which you cannot change or direct - you can only carry it around with you. Is that a good, serving choice for you?

There is a direct correlation between the degree to which you absorb other's energy forms by involvement in their lives and your own disempowerment.

Now revisit the question - how much are you involved in the dramas and happenings of the lives of others? You need to make a decision about how much of that is meaningful and serves good purpose, or how much you need to release and disconnect from? When you withdraw from such an energetic engagement, you will again clear a huge proportion of the busy-ness from your energy field. This is one of the primary aspects of learning to take command of your own life - making decisions about your involvement with others.

Support people in a strong and balanced way

There is of course, a balanced way for you to support, encourage and care for others in your life. It comes from your own place of inner balance, where your energy system is clear and flowing strong. In such a balanced state, you can assist another to see their way through troubles and difficulty in a compassionate and supportive way.

Your own awareness, and inner strength, can provide an energetic environment in which your interactions with others do not commence with the off-loading of their emotional debris on to you. With energy awareness, you will be able to manage the energy transactions without being drained or consumed on any level - physical, emotional or mental. Most importantly, the situations of others will no longer stir your own energy patterns and this will leave you in a commanding place of managing your own life more effectively.

As an advanced energy field healer, I have shared thousands of hours engaged in the lives of others on deeply emotional and painful levels. Quite literally, as a healer, my function is to enter and temporarily dwell within the woes of the World, because that's how energy healers transform such emotional pains and trauma. We engage with it energetically, then apply higher frequencies of energy to transform and heal the presence of trauma, pain and suffering. How do you think a healer would be able to do that every day, without becoming deluged and overwhelmed by such energy forms and patterns? What is it that keeps the healer balanced, light and capable of continuing such service to others?

A high quality and highly skilled healer knows how to clear, manage and maintain their own energy system. They know how to address and heal their own issues.

They know how to strengthen and maintain good strong flow in their own energy. Most essentially, they know how to consistently access the higher vibrations of love and compassion to fill their own life, with more than enough resource available to be effective at offering it to others also.

When I train my students in energy field healing techniques, the first thing they learn is how to clear energetic debris and forms from their own field. The Disconnection Command given in this chapter is one of the earliest things they take on board. The second thing they have to commit to, is clearing their own issues, because it is a healer's responsibility to ensure they are as clear and vibrant as possible to offer the service of healing to others.

Those two things alone, can make such a huge difference to the subtle energy content of your life. I have had the privilege of teaching Energy Field Healing to people from a wide variety of different professions - nurses, teachers, scientists, business people (managers, directors and entrepreneurs), writers, actors, psychologists, social workers, police officers, and a whole host of holistic therapists, carers and service providers. Their starting point is always the same - energy clearance.

These people from different walks of life are not necessarily training with me because they want to be full-time healers. They come because they know they need the knowledge in order to carry out their working service in a better and more effective way. They come to improve their quality of life and their ability to be self empowered in changing and creating the life they live. Subtle energy knowledge changes your overall view of life and highlights the purpose of living and sharing with others.

I believe we all know within that we are here for a higher purpose, that we are driven by the love within us to improve life and to serve the greater good of all. So we therefore only need to identify what is getting in the way of that higher purpose and generally, it's the lack of awareness of life's content that limits and constrains the glory of successful living.

I would like to share with you Melanie's story of the inspiration of her own life through discovering energy field healing. Melanie first met me in 1999 and was one of the students on the first ever Energy Field Healing training. She is South African born and had moved to London to develop her career just prior to the time she met me. She has the mind of a scientist, but the heart of a healer. She obtained her Bachelors Degree in Psychology and Anthropology in 1996 and within her career has gained considerable experience of working with disadvantaged communities, particularly the homeless and those with mental illness.

Over the years, Melanie has chosen to develop her inner purpose based on her understanding of energy field healing and subtle energies. I am proud to say she was one of the first I trained as a Teacher of Subtle Energy Awareness and she continues to create rich value in both her own life and the lives of others through her understanding and knowledge. Melanie offer's up her experience of discovering subtle energies and how it changed her life.

Hear Melanie's Story:

"I met Sue in 1999. She came to do an Energy Field Healing session for a co-worker who wasn't well. I had been working closely with this person in a live-in job at the time, I was working as a carer for those with disabilities. Following just that single session this person was just so much better. I watched amazed as her health improved and her life fell into place. I found out that Sue was about to start teaching a Diploma in Energy Field Healing and knew immediately on hearing about it that this was the course for me. I applied and was thrilled to be accepted. That was the beginning of a wonderful journey for me that is still continuing today!

I will always remember my first healing session with Sue. I had no idea what to expect but was very excited. We started the session and Sue asked me a simple question about whether I felt safe in life. The answer was no - since I was a child I had always felt unsafe in the world as if I always needed to look over my shoulder. I had just been used to feeling like this and thought that it was quite normal. During the session Sue healed an energetic pattern that related to this.

Since that session, I have never had that unsafe feeling return - even when I am in complicated situations, I always feel safe. To someone else that might have been invisible, but to me it was life changing. To have such a core feeling transformed was truly remarkable for me. It opened my eyes to the ability of this little known technique to change everything. To be able to change core feelings and transform them immediately and without distress was truly remarkable. I saw the possibilities there and became committed to being able to provide this service to others.

Sue helped me greatly in my personal healing sessions and readings that I was able to have with her. I have been lucky enough to attend a number of sessions with Sue, and now I often have healing sessions with her graduates, many of whom have exceptional skills themselves. Training with Sue has been an absolute honour. The Diploma course was life changing. The quality of Sue's teaching is unsurpassed - the clarity of information, the truthfulness and integrity of her teaching, and the sheer beauty of what is discovered on each course.

Sue teaches with intelligence and a sense of humour and when she tells you something it resonates deeply within you and you know it to be right. I feel I am able to trust what is said completely. Sue has incredible capacity to hold the energies of a group safely and provide what each person present needs. She plans the courses so beautifully that you feel the energy build before the course, sit in awe on the day, and leave feeling full of love, hope and joy. Each course heals and reconnects you to yourself.

I have attended a huge variety of courses with Sue in her venue in Birmingham over the years since the Diploma and have learned so much! The path has not always been easy as each step has brought new challenges and at times I have felt that I would never get something or make the next leap. It is wonderful to look back and see how much I have learned and grown.

Firstly Sue has helped me to learn how to manage my own energies... at this I am so much better. If something happens, I am able to gain insight quickly as to what is going on and bring light in. I notice that I feel much more well, physically, emotionally and mentally. My relationships have changed - family relationships and friendships are much easier and joyful. I have been able to find my life partner, and we are now joyfully married.

My heart feels open and I feel more in the moment and at peace. My skills have grown so much. In fact many of the skills that I have learnt and uncovered I never even imagined being able to do. I am able to feel the energy so clearly now. My skills around understanding and interpreting energy have grown exponentially.

I often see energy move and sometimes see incredible colours and hear harmonics. I can feel the movements of higher light around me every day. I have been able to get to know and communicate with my spirit guides and the angelic and other Beings who work with us unseen on a daily basis. To have this awareness inspires me very deeply and I am so grateful to Sue for helping me to learn how to work with them.

I am proud to have been able to open my own clinic in 2009 in London, and it has been a great joy to provide this service to clients myself. Many clients have reported back to me that they have seen remarkable changes even after the first session. Several clients have gone on to train with Sue and qualify as energy field healers themselves and it's wonderful to see the knowledge of this technique grow.

Energy awareness has fine-tuned my life skills, and in addition to healing people, homes and animals, I am now certified as an Inspirit Teacher, sharing Sue's teachings and know-how to others. I work in both London and Cape Town, South Africa, and it will be my absolute privilege to be of service to as many people as possible.

Sue has also developed over the years I have known her and recent courses have grown even more in scope and are bringing incredible understandings and learning about destiny, our origins, what's happening for humanity now. There is a sense of the energy awareness expanding into a greater arena. Understanding the sacred and universal laws and more about the energetic world in which we live, allows us to see everything from a new perspective.

We now have new skills to be able to work on a global level to bring change to the world and address the issues that we currently face. The potential for healing by using energy healing techniques in a rightful and loving way, is immense. I have taken part in some of the group work led by Sue and it has been an honour to be of assistance at this time in humanity's journey upon the Earth.

Sue lives what she teaches and is a fantastic example of how life can be lived differently. In all the time that I have known her she has never faltered on her path. She is incredibly patient, kind and strong. She has offered us, as a group of students and clients, absolute support and love throughout our journey. Sue has an incredibly loving and generous heart. I couldn't think of a better person to lead us forward with this higher awareness and understanding. I have enjoyed everything Sue and her spirit guides have ever brought to us and look forward to seeing how this new work will change people's lives and help to make the world a better place."

Melanie Stevens, Advanced Energy Field Healer,
Inspirit Teacher, and Meditation Facilitator

I appreciate Melanie sharing her story of discovery here. She is testimony to the fact that we can all come to learn about subtle energies and discover a useful and meaningful way to apply them. If we come to understand that within each and every one of us, there is a higher principle of living just waiting to burst out upon the world, then the only question is, how do we find it?

I can personally assure you that if you work to clear your own energies, you will be stronger and more capable of being a loving support to others, offering a greater contribution to life in general. You will be more aware of your reasons, your purpose and your motivations. Most particularly you will become aware of what is holding you back, limiting the quality of your life, and restricting the flow of your creativity and expression in the world. You can gain an awareness of what creates those times of demotivation, despondency, or just sheer incapacity to take action.

Learning the Disconnect Command and applying it regularly will help to keep your field clear. Adding some greater insight into how involved you are in the lives of others, will further clear space in your energy. And in that more open space... you will find the true you.

Now we're making space... real, clear, open space for new potential. Let's discover how to make that potential strong and optimal.

In Clear Space, We See More | 8

"With the creating of space comes a focus of vision. Be wise, do not move forward until you see."

So now we've brought some higher awareness to the flow of your energy transactions. You've made some choices about disconnecting and clearing out the energy forms and resonance that you do not wish to carry or absorb any longer. You have a little more space, which will be creating a clearer flow in your energy system and you will be more calm and focused.

Let's give a little more attention now to how we prepare that energy space for its best application in life, because surely, you want your next actions and ideas to be as empowered as possible, yes?

You can only ever be the highest potential of what is possible, based on your current energetic state.

It's important to understand that, because there is a mass of self-development material out in the world that states you can have "all you want" by just affirming, or demanding it, or willing it into the manifest world. That simply isn't true.

The only aspects of life that can manifest for you are those that can be attracted by your energetic state and condition. All life is based on the Law of Attraction and that law functions in consciousness, in energy, as like attracts like.

So, to achieve your desires, to live your passion, to acquire the success and wealth, or well-being that you desire, your starting point must be your current state of being - the condition of your own personal energy. If you do not address, heal and empower that, you cannot attract what you truly desire.

For the Law of Attraction to work in line with your will and desires, your current energetic state must be resonating at a matching frequency - the same energy resonance. That's the real secret... you can only ever be the highest potential of what is possible based on your current energetic state.

The filters of your perception

Your current energetic state dictates your perceptions, your processing ability, your filters and bias, your motivation and drive, your ability to feel and know truth. Your energy field is all around you, fully encompassing, so you see through it, you receive through it, you are always experiencing its essence.

You know the scenarios when you are feeling low and sad... everything you see in the world passes through that filter and you perceive the world with a low and sad bias. The opposite is also true. You will recognise the difference in your view of the world when you are bright, joyful and happy. We all recognise that we have bad days and good days. Surely though, we want to strive for the majority to be good days. Here's how to do it.

Raising your self-awareness of you the Being, of your life's experiences and circumstances, will inevitably bring to light your wounds. Everyone, at some stage in life, encounters emotional wound, pain, disappointment, humiliation, sadness or despair. It's part of the life process and we grow in consciousness as much from our pains as we do from our triumphs. As soul consciousness we are a continuing evolution of enhancement. From every facet of life experience, we will extract a lesson by which to grow.

One of two things has occurred with each life wound - either you have gained the value and knowledge, released the essence of it and moved on, or you are still carrying the energy forms within your energy field. These are either live and active, or dormant and waiting to erupt when triggered. Here are some indications that such a wound is present in your system:-

- If you find your thoughts often moving back in time and remembering hurtful circumstances and experiences of the past.
- If you can still hear the words someone said, or see the visions in your mind of how something painfully played out.
- If you still feel a powerful emotional response when you are reminded of something that happened years ago.
- If you still get an emotional surge when you see someone being affected by a similar painful experience that has happened to you.

In these scenarios, the 'wound' energies are still live and active and you are living under their influence. Whilst you carry such energies, your life's potential will be limited by their presence and your energy capacity will be lessened by the resonance of such wounds.

Wound energies are dense and within the field of energy, they lower the resonance of all other energies. The direct consequence is that even when you feel happiness, the shine of it soon fades, and even when a wholesome life experience occurs, it still leaves you feeling incomplete.

The presence of lower, dense energies within your field will always impact and influence your daily experiences. It has to be so - it is the only way the wounds can get your attention to their existence, in the hope you will heal them.

As a consciousness, you are always seeking to fulfil your highest potential. That is not possible if you are carrying aspects of life which lessen you. As a soul, you will endeavour to seek out life experiences which will bring your attention to that which needs transforming.

For the most part as humans, we play out our wounds through relationships - family, friends, partners and marriage. The more wounded we are, the more distressed our relationships. Wounded people, make wounded lives. Wounded parents make wounded children. Wounded lives create a wounded world.

If your life is full of distress, tragedy and despair; if there are excessive arguments, volatility and conflict; if things are continuously going wrong and you cannot achieve any of your desires, you need to look carefully at your energy state. Within your energy (consciousness) will be wounds that need transforming. Until you address that, life will continue to throw circumstances in your way to show you that something is imbalanced and non-serving. This is a function of intelligent consciousness.

Choosing to heal is the only true way

Making a conscious choice to clear and release old wounds is an empowered state. It's the point at which we say, "Enough is enough, I need life to be different". Making the commitment to make inner change will ultimately bring outer change. This is healing, this is growth.

You have a vast amount of resources available to you if you need supportive care, therapy or healing. Obviously, as a specialist in Energy Field Healing, I would recommend that to you and you can find out more about this innovative form of healing therapy on the website listed at the back of this book. But what matters most, is that you take some action to assist in revealing and transforming your past wounds.

The role and function of a healer is a simple one. We work with higher, lighter frequencies of energy in order to transform slower, denser frequencies of energy. That's what healing is - betterment created by transformation of energy resonance. For me, it is as much a science as it is an art. Working skilfully with the subtle energy system enables people to change.

The old wounds you are carrying fall into the category of dense energies. A skilled energy field healer will quickly be able to discover the patterns of those wounds in your energy system - they can be felt, 'read' and their essence 'interpreted', so that the resonance of a transformative higher energy can be applied.

Loving people to wellness

In healing, there are three main criteria essential to accessing and transforming a wound. First is acceptance, you have to acknowledge the experience and accept that it happened. This action opens the flow of the wound's energy form or pattern and reveals what occurred.

Second, is forgiveness. In my experience, I have observed that the majority of wounds remain present in the energy system because either one person or the other, or both/all involved, cannot forgive what has transpired. Both a lack of acceptance and a lack of forgiveness, lock the energy patterns of the wounds into place and there they remain, affecting all they come into contact with. Forgiveness is a higher virtue in energy resonance, its essence opens the energy to different potentials - higher potentials.

Finally within the healing process, we require love. Love, being the highest and fastest frequency of energy within universal source. Love does indeed, heal all things. This is the primary function of the healer, to become a conduit for the flow of that universal energy. Since the healer is neutral within the process, it is possible for them to bring love to you, to others involved, to the situation and circumstances of the wound. The truth is, as healers, we love people into wellness.

The application of the higher frequencies of energy will transform the dense energy forms. The energy flows are 'lightened', and energy forms that were blocking or lessening the natural flow of the energy system will begin to release from the field. The energy form of the wound is no longer present and, therefore, a new potential becomes available in the energy system.

A highly skilled, sensitive and confidential healer can be one of the most enhancing services you ever choose to engage with. When making your choice remember the basic principles necessary for a high quality healer. Let me guide you on this because if you are unfamiliar with healing, you may not understand the skills or standards you should seek.

Choosing a high quality healer:

The healer should be physically well with buoyant and strong energy. A healer who is unwell will not be able to be a conduit for the array of higher frequencies of energy required for transformation. That's just basic physics. Physical illness indicates an imbalanced, blocked or weakened energy system and/or the presence of dense energy. That means the healer will most likely be more in need of the healing energy than the client. A highly skilled and knowledgeable healer will never offer their service when they are unwell, because they would know they can only provide a lesser quality to the client because they have their own needs to meet.

The healer's kindness and loving commitment to your well-being should be obvious and felt by you, right from your first introduction. The warmth and safety you sense with a good quality healer is the nature and essence of their energy. You should be able to sense this immediately upon meeting.

The words they speak to you should always be kind, supportive and enhancing. Healing is a high-frequency activity and therefore those higher aspects of heart energy are engaged - kindness, love, compassion, grace, beauty. That's what should be flowing out of the healers mouth and into your presence in order to strengthen, support and empower you.

The healer should be completely confidential and trustworthy. You should be able to feel at ease to share your innermost concerns, pains and traumas.

Your healing session is for you and about you. If you encounter a healer who starts talking about their own issues, or starts chatting about things that do not relate to you or your life experiences - leave! Such a person is not honouring the sacredness and security of the healing space that should be dedicated only to your well-being.

Your healer should have absolute respect for the sacredness of the art of healing. If they dramatise, gossip, or expect you to adapt to their 'way', then they are not holding the higher vibration of virtuous grace that will bring you healing transformation.

Healing is a sacred art, it honours a higher code of spiritual law. When that sacred art is truly within someone you will see it on the outside, because it is so beautifully present on the inside.

A personal referral is always best

When you seek the services of a healer, allow your intuition to guide you. Try to make a discerning choice based on another's recommendation of a high quality of service.

Consider how you would employ any other trade or service and don't bypass common sense requirements, because you feel you are seeking an unusual or alternative service. There is nothing mystical, magical or supernatural about a true, good quality healer. A highly skilled healer will have worked at, and earned, their value and service abilities.

The best route to a good quality healer is by recommendation. The proof of healing ability is in the results and when people get results, they recommend.

That's a far safer route than believing any sales or marketing hype, or self-proclaimed achievements on the part of the healer. The first place people go now for services and products is the internet. Any professional healer, who is offering their work of service as their main livelihood, will have representation on the internet. Look for others' testimonials on the healer's website. When people are happy with a service, they are willing to offer up testimonial to encourage others to gain the value they have.

A genuine, high quality healer will be getting good results for clients. The reputation for that will quickly spread. I found that within a short time of commencing my clinic, personal recommendations had created a mass of bookings and people were having to wait up to six months for an appointment. With a developing reputation for high level skills, I quickly became known as 'the healers' healer' and healers and therapists throughout the region were coming to see me for the maintenance of their own well-being. So, look for the presence of good reputation when you seek to develop a supportive and caring relationship with a healer.

Healing is a sacred art, the skills we healers hold and with which we serve, are a privilege. It saddens me to have heard over the years of the encounters that some have experienced with lower quality so-called healers. In all fields of life though, you find the extremes of quality and skill level. A few will be high quality with exceptional skills; many will be at the mid-level range of offering good service; and some will be at the low quality end of the scale. That's how it is in every arena of life.

So, make a discerning choice and use your common sense, to gain the help and support you need. Within the field of healing, truth and integrity are everything, because they are the higher principles of consciousness. Look for those higher principles in your healer, because then you can be assured they are a conduit for the higher presence of source.

Self healing as an alternative

If you would prefer to work with self-healing and revealing and transforming your own issues, then maybe you would like to use the following procedure as a guide. There will sometimes be occasions when something is too painful, or the wound is too severe for you to be able to deal with it yourself. Most of life's general issues though can be supported and transformed with a little care and attention from yourself.

Guide to Self Healing inner wounds:

Ensure you have some good quiet time in which to explore your inner feelings. Your objective is to access the original energy form of your wound or distress, and interruptions or noise will distract you from the level of concentration you need. Settle down, become quiet and still. Close your eyes to cease any further inflow of visual data. Focus on the issue that has arisen or been triggered.

Start by asking "How do I feel about this?". Your objective is to access the underlying core feeling by moving through the mask of all the other feelings that have covered up the deeper issue.

If you stay with the primary question and let the energy flow with your intention to uncover and reveal the truth, then ultimately, you will access the original energy form of the wound.

You have two options with this exercise. You can either re-engage with the experience, or you can position yourself as a 'spectator' and review what occurred. If the wound is too painful for you to feel comfortable about re-engaging with it, then choose to be a 'spectator'. That means you can review what happened, but not have to re-experience the emotions that were involved. This is a method of consciousness positioning, which you can achieve by directive intent.

Your mind will be recalling memories and showing you the story line, which runs a little like a video recording of the event in your 'mind's eye'. What is actually happening is that your consciousness is revisiting the memory patterns and energetic forms of that experience. Sometimes the visuals may appear out of time sequence and images may seem to be random. On other occasions, your visuals may just take you directly to the origin of the issue.

Once the story line is revealed, you can make a choice to start transforming the energy forms and patterns of that issue, by applying healing intent. Remember the three key healing principles:

- Acceptance/acknowledgement
- Forgiveness - of self and others
- Love

You need to allow a little time for the energies to transform and release. You will experience this in your own way, but it is common for people to 'see' white or golden light as the causal event seems to lift up and dissipate. Sometimes people 'see' flashes of light and then feel the release. Ultimately, what does matter, is that you FEEL a change in what this issue means to you. Once a wound is transformed through healing, the energy 'charge' is taken out of it and therefore it cannot impact you in the same way ever again.

Please do exercise care and common sense when choosing self-healing. You should always seek professional advice and medical care in managing your health and well-being. The technique given above is complementary to any professional medical care you receive, not a substitute for it. There is enormous benefit in life to releasing and transforming old wounds and emotional difficulties. Not only will it free your energy to flow stronger and with renewed source, but your views and perceptions of life will change because you are no longer viewing the world through the filter of those wounds.

Developing visualisation techniques

My next recommendation to you would be to learn to visualise. The benefits of both visualisation and meditation are well documented and in support of developing higher awareness, they are essential to include in your healing and self-development programme.

Visualisation is the skill of working pro-actively with mindful intent whilst in an expansive state of consciousness. Your relaxed and open state of consciousness connects into higher potentials, so anything you visualise or create within that state becomes enhanced. Visualisation is ideal for achieving greater understanding of anything, including people, relationships, events, situations, choices, creations, unexpected circumstances and even undesired outcomes.

Visualisation is very different from meditation. It is also very different from relaxation. The first products I personally created were CD's for guided meditation because I was inundated with questions from people about how to develop these skills. I created my own as I discovered that I couldn't recommend to people anything already available, because the visualisation CD's had background music on them and would most likely be more effective at offering relaxation, than actual visualisation. Once background music is present, it engages the brainwaves in aligning to the harmonics of the music. The mind may not then be free to expand and connect into the higher intelligence that resides within expansive consciousness.

Please don't misunderstand me, relaxation and methods for relaxation, are very useful and will serve you well. Music on such CD's will help to calm your mind because the brainwaves will synchronise with the musical harmonics. That may relax you, and that's a good thing. However, in terms of the brainwave frequencies needed, relaxation is different to visualisation. And visualisation is different to meditation. Both visualisation and meditation are best achieved in quietness.

Meditation is achieved through a deep state of expansive consciousness and requires silence. As you expand your energies to connect into higher awareness, the potential for communion with source becomes available. Meditation is so deeply restorative because it connects us with primary source energy. It helps to balance the mind and the emotions, and restore the spirit.

Use visualisation when you want to explore and develop understanding of life circumstances, ideas, situations, difficulties, challenges and so on. It is an ideal way to 'view' what is actually occurring and what solutions may be available.

Visualisation is also ideal for bringing source energy (higher light) into your creations and for helping to manifest in the physical world. There is a flood of material on the global marketplace which tries to teach you how to manifest. Different techniques from 'calling' things to you, 'demanding' things, making constant affirmation to conjure them into being and so on. Really, creation and manifestation isn't that difficult when you come to understand it as a higher principle of life. The moment you realise that what manifests is a product of the subtle energy factors present, then your ability to understand your life process changes and your choices about creating for the better can start to enact.

You can also use visualisation techniques to pre-position positive and serving outcomes for your future happenings and events. Directing higher source energy and light into future events can assist you on all levels to achieve greater serving outcomes.

One of the first visualisations I teach my students is called the 'Show me, Me'. It's an exercise that calms the mind and establishes a higher intelligence connection, where the student asks "Show me, Me". In the visualisation, they will see an image of themselves and the flow of their own subtle energy. From that they can detect where the energies are weak, congested or imbalanced, and what needs healing or attention to support their personal growth.

This technique is designed to assist the student in discovering aspects of their own health and well-being which they need to tend to, in order to become a clear conduit for the higher frequency energies needed to heal others. In the visualisation they may see images of past scenarios, or childhood events, in fact, anything that needs its story revealed in order for them to be energetically clear and strong.

Over the years, I have developed many unique guided visualisations to help people heal and journey safely through their clearance of the past. I have also designed forward-development visualisations to help empowerment, creation and the fulfilment of enhanced living and manifesting. If you are interested in using visualisation as a life tool, you can find details at the end of this book about the 'Enhance your Light ~ Enhance your Life' Visualisation Programme, which I developed for the public from the very best of the techniques taught to my students over more than a decade.

I have outlined to you the benefits of quiet time, self healing and visualisation. If you are able to make these a regular part of your weekly energy maintenance programme, you will rapidly improve and enhance the quality of your life. Receiving the higher flows of source energy into your field will sustain your higher functions and you will find that on every level, you are becoming more capable and more in command.

"Having an understanding of the movement of subtle energies around us, and the people we live and work with, has completely turned my life around for the better. I have learned how people can empower you, and at the same time, how some can disempower you. However, the difference is, I can see why people can be dis-empowering, whether it be from a wounded past, conditioning, patterns that affect them or any other underlying issue. As a result, I have learned to view them through the eyes of compassion and grace, and am able to bring light to them.

We have so many energy transactions each day with the people and places we come into contact with. Using simple techniques to clear and stabilise my energies, and clear my personal and work space, has enabled me to live my life full of energy and enthusiasm. I am able to keep my energies high and light, which has a positive effect on all those I come into contact with. This has had a great impact on my family and my work as a school teacher.

Subtle energies do exist, we all sense and feel things. By using energy management techniques, we can all be more empowered to manage these and hence manage our lives in a much more positive way. I did!"

A. Jeetley, Science Teacher and Certified Teacher of
The Subtle Energy Awareness Programme®

Get Yourself Together | 9

"Dispersed across time and place, and non-directive in our intent. No wonder we can't make our way forward."

Let me explain a little more about what happens to your outward flowing energies on a daily basis. You are coming to understand now that your energy is you as a flow of consciousness. How you apply your mindfulness and intent each day will dictate how well you manage, how empowered you are and how content you will feel at the end of that day.

Remember always that the energy will flow with your intent, so you must maintain awareness of how you apply your directive thinking. Throughout the day, your thoughts and feelings are going to move you into different time and space. As you become emotionally engaged with any matter you will invest aspects of your consciousness to connect to it.

A simple example of this may be - on this day you are involved in organising a party for a family member, a special party which will take place in two weeks time. Your mind travels back to the time and place of the last great family party you had a couple of years ago. You see in your mind the location, the room, remember the laughter and singing. You focus on the highlights of that party, what went well, the surprises, who was thrilled, and so on. Whilst your mind is reflecting upon that, your energy has moved back into past time, back into the location (space), reconnected with those people you brought to mind and most importantly, you are re-feeling emotions you experienced during that event.

Simultaneously, your mind is projecting forward to the party which is to take place two weeks hence. So you have also moved into future time, you are connecting to a different location, you will be connecting to those people who will or will not be there, you are considering all the arrangements and details. Your mind might connect to the caterer, or the gift supplier, and whoever is providing other services. You will be feeling a whole array of emotions based on the tone and essence of everything that has occurred in relation to the intended event. You also have the emotional investment in what you would like to occur and the desired outcome - your hopes for a happy occasion.

These movements in time and space are occurring whilst you still hold your activities in the 'now' moment, whilst dealing with all the present busy-ness. Do you see now that actually, there are a multitude of energy connections of thoughts, intentions, feelings and actions connected to just a single event or experience. Now, let's amplify that based on the busy nature of life.

You are always energetically moving in time and space

In any given hour you will connect to multiple places, projects, people, time zones (past/future/now), ideas, concepts, communications, feelings, responses, reactions, intentions and memories. All these aspects connect as energy forms or patterns, an energy flow driven by a purpose in consciousness and the momentum of their motivations. You are a very active human being on a subtle energy level.

Consider for a moment, how busy are your days? How many people do you communicate with or become involved with? How many places do you visit - work, shops, home, others' homes, clients? How many tasks do you tend? How many plans do you make? How many functions have to occur to maintain the flow of your manifest physical life? That's a general description of anyone's life on a usual daily basis. Imagine the intensity when we increase the energy transactions, or become involved in higher priority projects or situations.

All this activity moves your energy continuously into multiple space and time zones. If you are able to manage and command your energy well, you will be able to reclaim the outward flows of your personal energy fully to your Core Centre and fully into the 'now' moment regularly throughout the day.

However, if you remain unaware of these energy movements, the outcomes and consequences can be very different. The majority of people do not realise they are expending energy outwards with every life activity. As such, they will continue to operate in their state of busy-ness, until they just simply run out of energy. Then they are tired, exhausted and unable to function.

People have a tendency to over-stretch their resources. If you continue at a rate that exceeds your capacity to manage, then on an energetic level, you will not be able to command the reclaiming of the outward flowing energies into your core energy system. In energy terms, I call this dispersal - your energy becomes dispersed, connected into various places and caught up in differing times zones of past and future. You would recognise this as being 'out of sorts' or 'scatty', or 'all over the place'. You might even hear yourself saying that.

When your energy is overly dispersed, and this is a common state, the effects are obvious. It can create pressure in the head (headache) and fatigue. You may become clumsy, dropping things, bumping into things, losing things. You may get disorientated and head in the wrong direction. Ever had those times when you go into a room and then cannot recall what you went in there for? What about times of so called 'absent mindedness' - you get off the lift on the wrong floor, get on the wrong bus, take a wrong turn on a route you regularly travel?

How do you think the mind could become absent? That's energy dispersal. If it continues, you lose focus on timings and start running late. You will forget obvious things and become easily distracted. You become disorganised and find yourself saying... "That's not like me to...", "I don't usually...".

If you continue in a dispersed state for any length of time, exhaustion will ensue, a complete feeling of being drained. When your energy is scattered in different zones of time and space, your own energy flow and balance cannot be maintained. You will feel the stress levels rise within you and your energies will be out of flow and sequence.

You cannot live an empowered life in a dispersed state. In such a condition, you are not fully in command of your life flow, and are therefore open to and subject to, the circumstances and dramas that occur as a consequence. It is likely that you will be living a reactive life having to 'do' what everyone else is asking of you.

There's some great news here for all who feel dispersed, too often. Your energy is yours, it's your consciousness, therefore it can be reclaimed by your command. A simple statement of command will reclaim for you a considerable degree of the energies you have scattered. Here is the command we use to reclaim dispersed energies, it is said with directive intent.

The 'Reclaim Command'

"I RECLAIM ALL MY PERSONAL ENERGIES THAT IT SHALL SERVE MY HIGHEST PURPOSE TO RECLAIM AT THIS TIME. RECLAIMING NOW."

Let me just add a key point to your skill of reclaiming. Please refer once again to the previous pictures of the energy field. You will see the point in the middle of the abdomen that I refer to as 'Core Centre'.

When you are reclaiming your energies, have your focus directed upon the Core Centre - place your hands there if you need to. Your intent should be to reclaim your energies fully to your Core Centre and in the energy system, that is where it's positioned.

When people talk about "being centred" this is what they are referring to. Your Centre is the optimal place of power and balance for your energy system, it's essential that it is strong and stable. The Core Centre is the place within the energy system where all lines of energy dynamics enter you, the physical being. It's the power place, the central power 'junction' for your energy system.

The Reclaim Command is a simple technique, but I can assure you it will work. The energy will always flow with your intent. If you lead a particularly busy life you should actively use the energy management skills of Disconnection (given in Chapter 7) and Reclaiming. They are invaluable simple tools to manage your energy and can be applied morning, afternoon and night. It will take just a couple of minutes to focus and make your command with mindful intent.

Over the years of teaching these simple commands, I have received masses of feedback from students and clients about their success and empowerment from applying such simple energy management skills.

It works for me too. I personally lead a very busy life. I manage three businesses and care for and support hundreds of students and clients. I have a family and home to manage also. People have so often asked me how I manage to 'do' so much. My answer... I manage the energy flows. I don't have stress because I know how it arises and can clear it immediately from the energy. I don't get involved in anything (past, present or future) that does not truly need my assistance or attention. And most importantly, I've cleared and transformed the emotional and mental energy forms that I carried through life, up to the point I discovered healing and energy skills. Energy management is life management.

The Reclaim Command will return to your own space, the aspects of your energies that are dispersed. It will bring them to centre, and return them fully to the 'now moment' - which is essential for your strength and focus. The only truly empowered moment you have is that of 'now'. Most importantly, the reclaimed energies will re-fuel you - quite literally, you are reclaiming your own energy resources that should not be dispersed elsewhere. Once reclaimed, you have that energy fuel once again available as a resource, you have boosted your capacity. Exhaustion should not then occur, because your energy management system is firmly in place and operating efficiently.

When you understand that you are expending your energies outwards, whilst simultaneously receiving incoming energies from others, you begin to see the two-way exchange occurring - like an energy currency exchange. Living daily on a basis of expending more energy than you receive creates a deficit, an energetic imbalance that will have consequences to your well-being. So be wise and use the Reclaim Command to re-energise your system accordingly.

The techniques of disconnection and reclaiming should keep your energy stable. It will limit the amount of energetic non-serving influence incoming from other people, because you have cleared the attracting elements and connections. Reclaiming helps to maintain your energy resources, which means you have more capacity to manage the many 'doings' of your daily life. Most especially, your energy will be more cohesive, flowing with ease and power.

Let me share with you Bernadette's story. Leading a very busy life with a pressurised career, Bernadette was unaware until discovering subtle energies, that her daily activity was building on top of all the past activity still flowing through her system. Feeling the 'heaviness' of her life, she had come to learn to live with the way things were, not knowing there was a way to clear it out and get her life into order.

Hear Bernadette's Story:

"I had a gradual introduction to energy field healing, firstly as a client receiving healing from Sue. Feeling the immense benefits, it eventually steered me

to studying Energy Field Healing to advanced level during 2011/2012. My realisation about this was that it isn't just another form of healing available. It isn't just about healing, it is about managing my day to day energy transactions to keep myself clear of all the 'invisible clutter' that led me to receive healing in the first place.

For several years I had felt bogged down, heavy, emotional, fatigued. I felt as though I had no control over my life and as much as I tried, I couldn't completely put things right. My first session of energy field healing was very powerful. I was surprised at how different I felt and in the coming months, noticed the release of such heavy invisible burdens. I was also very surprised at the amount of information that came out during my healing session which explained some of the reasons why I had such a difficult time. Basically I was hooked in to events from the past, as a child and adult, which I had not released. Hence the reasons for my repeating patterns of the 'same old stuff' over and again.

In January 2011 my partner and I became the legal guardians of a 5 year old girl, who came to us with her own issues and experiences for one so young. It was very hard to deal with her emotional outbursts as we didn't always know what caused them, alongside having to deal with the external factors that influenced her life. At this time I was in the early stages of understanding energy transactions, but had learned enough from my healing experience and Sue's workshops to recognise that our child's behaviour was more than just an expression of 'bad behaviour'. I knew she was in need of support that went beyond the conventional understanding.

I made an appointment for our child to attend one of the specialist clinics Sue organised for children. My little girl was quite interested and very well behaved during her healing and I remember how very detailed and complicated her session was. She only had to lay on the comfy couch, oblivious to what was going on around her. I was learning to understand the mother/child relationship and how those factors were hooked in to her, resulting in these emotional outbursts that she couldn't explain afterwards. It gave me a clear insight into different ways of dealing with her behaviour as opposed to just assuming I had a very naughty child that needed to be chastised each time she threw a strop.

After the healing session, my child slept for the rest of the afternoon and I noticed a great improvement in her attitude and behaviour towards us. It wasn't perfect but gradually got better as the healing process continued. I also arranged for my child to have distant healing when things were getting a little difficult for her. Those external factors that were affecting her well-being were given healing and that helped to release a lot of the tension she was feeling.

We also decided to have an energy cleansing on our house to remove stagnant energy that had accumulated over time. We had started to notice what we described as spooky stuff going on. Although the house didn't feel haunted, it started to feel very heavy. I wasn't comfortable going upstairs, it felt totally different to downstairs, and I would wake in the night feeling very anxious.

One Sunday two advanced energy field healers came to our house and stayed for most of the day. They cleared so much debris and they described the energy imbalances that were allowing external energies to come and go, causing disruption. Past energies from previous occupants were also cleared and all I can say is what a relief.

My partner and I noticed a complete change in the feel of our house. I could only describe it as quiet. Although there was no audible sound before the healing, the house had felt busy and chaotic. After the healing it was quiet, peaceful and balanced. One very obvious improvement was in our child's moods, she calmed down after the home healing and was not as hyper-active as before.

I convinced my partner to have energy field healing to clear the debris he was carrying that I could see was affecting him. He was open to the suggestion although blasé about it but, had a healing session that was very insightful. What still astounds me is how family links can affect our lives and even more astounding, how energy field healing along those energy lines can clear a huge amount of burden. My partner thoroughly benefitted from his healing session and has subsequent healing when he needs it.

When I studied the Diploma in Energy Field Healing I learned self-cleansing techniques, disconnection and energy protection techniques. I continue to receive periodic healing to keep myself clear and well and can honestly say I don't know how I would have lived my life going forward without the knowledge that I now have. I have a very busy life, full of challenges and happenings, but a basic energy command during the day can make me feel different within minutes. Energy awareness has been invaluable to me and I am so grateful that I came across it at a time when I really needed it.

I know that without energy field healing and without my understanding of day to day energy transactions, I would not be the person that I am now. I recently spent one-to-one time with Sue for a session she calls 'subtle life mapping'. We discussed where I'd like to work, where we'd like to live, whether I am on the right path to achieving my ambitions and the challenges to overcome in order to achieve my mission. I still find visualisation difficult, but with Sue's help and skills at 'reading', we put together a life map to clear away some of the difficulties and barriers to moving forward. By the time my life map was complete it was a rainbow of colours and I keep looking at it and it links me right into where I should be heading and I can feel such positive change ahead for me."

Bernadette Smith, Civil Servant (Education Sector)
& Advanced Energy Field Healer,

Bernadette's story outlines what is so common for the majority of people - without an understanding of how life transactions build up in your system energetically, you are missing a major part of understanding the management of your life. Her experience of discovering the usefulness and application of subtle energy techniques is not uncommon. Once people realise that there is a way to make change by applying easy to learn skills, they come to understand the value of their own ability to be empowered to do so.

Every step of the way, subtle energy awareness helps you develop a greater understanding of your life and all that you connect into on those subtle invisible levels. It's the equivalent of having the 'insider story' of every relevant part of your life. That's powerful, that's engaging and it's a masterful way to approach the living of your life.

The information in this book is your starting point, the point from which you can begin to make a real difference in your life. There are a multitude of highly technical and sophisticated aspects to the structure and flow of subtle energy fields. Such knowledge could probably fill volumes of an encyclopedic nature and I would probably lose your attention just part of the way through. Unless you have a need for such technical knowledge, you would not venture to study it. Perhaps a bit like studying quantum physics, most of us do not have a need for it in everyday life and therefore wouldn't venture the time and resources to understand it.

So I offer to you as much as is reasonable in order to make your life more manageable by gaining insight to subtle energies. For me however, the study of the human energy field and the flows and connectivity of subtle energies has become my life's work. I have witnessed too many exceptional cases of positive change and enhancement, to not realise the true value of subtle energy awareness.

Movement within time and space is one of the more complex functions of consciousness, yet we engage in it every day without even realising its implications. Time - as an energy, as a flow, as an aspect of consciousness that creates our history - is both compelling and fascinating. The way time flows through the energy field and how it affects our individual perception of life is enthralling to me. How we move within time in our consciousness is equally fascinating.

Timing and its synchronisation with the higher purpose of life, is everything. It's how you meet that person at just the right time, be there in the right place for that moment of opportunity, say or do just the right thing at exactly the moment that offers the best outcome. Timing is everything and it only flows in synchronicity in a clear, balanced and cohesive energy field.

Have you wondered why time occasionally seems to just flow right by when you're engaged in something interesting or joyful? Or indeed, why it 'drags' and passes by slowly when you're doing something you dislike or resent? Those perceptions of time relate to the speed and resonance of the energy flow of your field. When you are feeling light and joyous (in a high frequency state) the time passes by quickly, because the vibration within your field is higher and faster. Quite literally, time flies by when you're having fun!

When you are encountering slow and dense feelings (a lower frequency state) the time appears to slow down. That's because aspects of time flow through the interweave of your subtle energy layers. When they are in a state of dense energy, it literally slows down the perception of the passing of time.

Your perception of time is directly relational to the resonance of your energy state. So, clear your energy field into a high frequency state and then you can truly enjoy all the time you have!

"Energy Field Healing has changed my life. I first started studying it eight years ago with Sue Zange. I have experienced some pretty turbulent things in both my personal and working life. Having the knowledge of how subtle energy works has helped me through these experiences and enabled me to comprehend why certain life events happen and what I learn from it, as well as how to apply the healing to whatever has happened.

I work as a nurse, often caring for frail elderly patients. What's reassuring is that through using energy field healing I can create a stable, loving, healing environment for every patient. This radiates out to all the staff working with them as well. Many of my colleagues often comment on my calmness and I'm known within my team as the one who keeps everyone balanced.

I would never hesitate to recommend subtle energy knowledge to anyone. It makes a beautiful difference to your life and to others."

L. Fulford, Registered Nurse &
Advanced Energy Field Healer

The Power of the Ground | 10

"We are designed to be upon the Earth, we should let it nourish and nurture us in the way it was truly intended."

Grounding is our next important matter to address in order to maintain stable energy. The term 'grounding' refers to how well you anchor your own personal energy into the ground (the Earth).

You will see from previous diagrams how the energy radiates out around you and all the way down below your feet. The flow of energy beneath your feet connects into the natural electro-magnetic field of the Earth. In this way, your flow of energy combines with the earth's flow of energy - it is the place you belong. The energy that radiates up from the ground is a natural range of frequencies of energy that we use as resource. It feeds and fuels us and helps maintain a strong energy system. It is particularly vital for physical health.

Good grounding connection serves in multiple ways:

- It anchors our energy at the base of the main axis, and therefore, we are positioned more stable in space (location).
- A deep ground connection enables more source energy to flow up into our energy field (through the 'Earthstar' energy centre), so sustaining our well-being.
- Heightened charge and over-activity in the energy can be easily discharged to ground by applying intent.

I would like to explain that last point a little further. Through the multitude of energy transactions occurring for you each day, there will be some that hold a 'heightened charge'. Those are times when the emotional and mental energies are charged up through anger, aggravation, provocation, distress, panic and so on. Or maybe the times when something is overly important to you, when there is a lot 'at stake' upon the outcome. These are times when you can easily lose command of your emotions, your actions and the rationale of your thought process, due to such heightened charge and activity in the energy.

Two of the primary catalysts which send the energy into 'heightened charge' are fear and shock. At various times in life, we will all encounter our crisis moments. This may be when something actually shocking occurs, which sends us into emotional and mental turmoil. Or it may be when something triggers a fear response within us. There will be times when fear courses through each of us as a response to a life experience. Often, our immediate uncontrolled response to fear is expressed through anger and outburst.

On these occasions the energies surge within your system, they gather an immense momentum within and around you - force. Due to the nature of the conflicting emotions you hold within your system, the energies start to powerfully 'bounce around', creating what I refer to as a 'heightened charge'. Basically, you've become an uncontrollable mass of colliding energy forms.

At times, that charge will burst out of you, directed towards something or someone, venting as anger, hostility or even violence. Alternatively, it could implode upon you, reducing you to tears and blubbering and a sense of being beaten or defeated.

Once you become aware of your energetic state, you will learn to recognise the times you are heading towards heightened charge. You should take action to command your energies before they reach an uncontrolled state.

The ground can absorb heightened charge

The safest and easiest way to discharge 'heightened energy charge' is to the ground. This is done through a visualisation process and use of the breath, to calm the energies and 'send them to ground' with your intent. It is an easy technique to apply because you are already connected to the ground energies through your field. The only issue is whether you think to apply the technique when heading towards that heightened charge state.

Discharging excess, heightened, or chaotic energies to ground is a powerful self-management tool. So long as you recognise those times when the energy charge is rising within and around you, then you can take action to manage it. Remaining in command requires you to notice and be aware of escalating energy states, so that you manage and change them before they overwhelm you.

Fear can trigger within you unexpectedly if you are carrying dense, unhealed wounds and issues in your energy. Don't put yourself at the mercy of their capacity to bewilder you. Make a better choice.

The key here is self-awareness - to know when your energies are beginning to feel imbalanced, dense or 'charged up'. There may be the occasional crisis situation that takes you unaware, but for the most part, you can manage a great deal more with awareness. Bear in mind that you are more vulnerable to 'heightened charge' situations if your energies are already unstable. The more stable you are, the more aware you are. Then you are more in command of managing the incoming life events.

During my years in the healing clinic, I cared for hundreds of powerful people in top level jobs, who consistently were encountering high-powered situations, where there was a lot 'at stake'. They would come to see me regularly in order to keep their energy field clear and balanced, because they knew it made them less vulnerable to the circumstances of their environments. A clear and balanced energy field will always strengthen your position in whatever area of work you are involved and it will limit your vulnerability to 'heightened charged' scenarios.

I have also been involved in a considerable amount of 'crisis management' scenarios, where the event has happened and clients need me to come in and re-stabilise the energies, calm the effects and rebuild the subtle energy foundations, so that things can move forward in the right direction. I consider one of the most powerful skills of subtle energy management is the ability to manage and transform a crisis and re-direct the future potentials to a more acceptable outcome.

Maintaining subtle energy awareness and self-awareness, means that you do not have to become reactive in life circumstances. It is best to not get to that place of vulnerability in which a life happening can send you into chaos and distress. I am sure everyone will be able to relate to what I am referring to as 'heightened charge'.

Think of all the times you've had sudden outbursts - anger, rage, hostility, panic, or tears. Or the scenarios where you just cannot stop yourself 'venting' or 'getting something out of your system' and you rage at someone or something? Those times when you are 'pushed over the edge'.

What about the times you purposely have to go out or do some kind of activity to 'let off steam'? What do you think that 'steam' is? It's heightened charge in the energy within your field. Think about the times you have been in arguments or conflict with people and how het-up the entire situation became. Did it get out of control? Did you say or do things you later regretted because you were out of control? All these scenarios lead to misunderstanding, miscommunication, break down in relationship and potentially, further destructive actions or even violence.

Keep calm and stabilise your energy

Maintaining a clear energy field is the primary way to remain calm, no matter what the situation. So, if you are now starting to adopt some energy management techniques to stabilise the flow of your energy, the next skill that needs to be in your awareness is your ground connection.

It's powerful. Your emotional and mental stability depend on a stable and deep ground connection. That connection will be a clearance vent for you whenever you need to discharge excess energies that are flowing through you.

So, how do we achieve a good strong ground connection? Once again, you need to acknowledge and apply the power of your intent. Now that you are learning awareness of your energy field, you have the power to direct its flow.

When you are learning to develop a deeper ground connection, the best place to do so is outside, with your feet on natural earth. Most people have a garden, others I have trained make use of the park or countryside. You're looking to achieve a direct connection to the Earth rather than a 'synthetic' connection through a concrete floor of a building.

If you cannot be outside, then let me mention at this stage that developing a good ground connection requires you to at least be at ground level. As buildings ascend in storeys up from the ground, the actual power of the ground energy lessens. It is very weak by 3-4 storeys up, so at that height, it will not fuel you well. As humans, we are not really designed to be off the ground. It's thought provoking when you consider our modern world of city skyscrapers where many work and/or live, high off the ground.

Preferably, you need to cultivate a good relationship with the Earth. Get out into nature and really connect with it - don't just watch it, actually connect.

Method to Ground your Energy

1. You require about 10-15 minutes to focus on good grounding.
2. Stand on the Earth, fully upright, preferably without shoes.
3. Visualise and bring your focus to your energy field around you.
4. Purposely focus on the layers of energy beneath your feet and 'see' them going deep into the ground.
5. Bring your focus to the vertical central axis of energy that flows through you, and visualise it flowing down through your centre, down between your legs, reaching deeply into the Earth.
6. Visualise the excess/non-serving energy filtering away to ground. 'See' it going downwards, apply your intent to send it to ground and let the Earth absorb it away from you.

When a good connection is made to the ground, two things occur. Firstly, you will feel as though the energy debris and heightened charge in your system is just flowing away and you will instantly feel lighter and more calm. Secondly, you will get a sensation as though you are sinking into the ground a few inches, or that the ground is coming up to meet you. At that stage, you can be sure that you have merged your energy fully into the ground energies and you will be receiving greater sustenance and stability.

Let nature support your energy

The Earth is our home, so developing a relationship with nature makes sense. The more connected you feel to the ground, the stronger will be your sense of belonging. The advantages of developing your relationship with the Earth are many. First and foremost, a deeper connection means more ground source energy is flowing into your field to fuel you. As a direct result, you will have more power and strength of flow in your energy field. More power and strength means greater capacity for life activities. It also provides a fresh, new supply of energy any time you begin to feel fatigued or low on fuel.

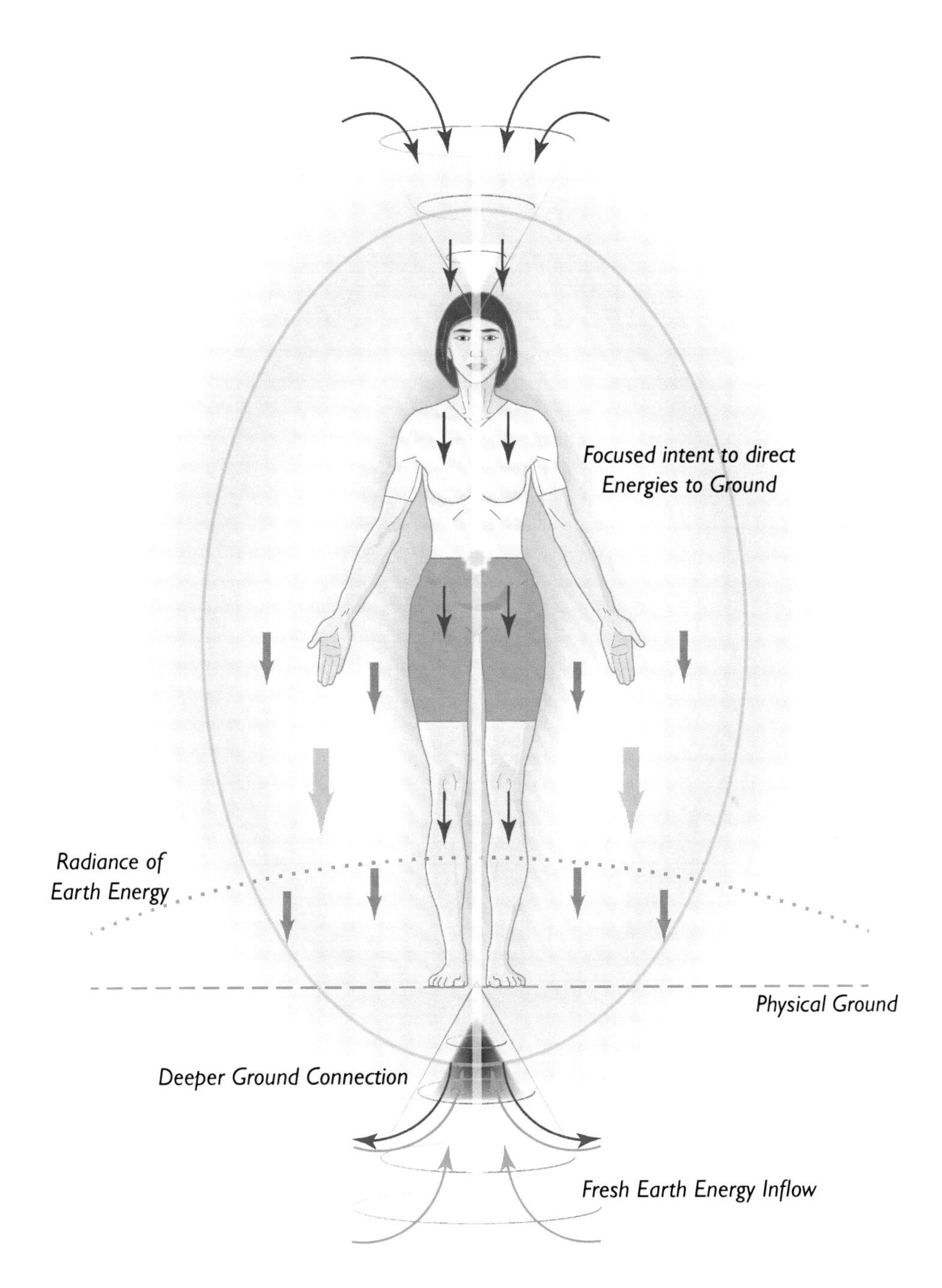

Picture 7 - Using intent to discharge Energies to Ground

As a secondary benefit, the process of connecting with the Earth re-ignites our communion with nature, we begin to feel more at-one with the World. That has obvious benefits in terms of appreciating our environment and being grateful for the life sustaining resources the Earth offers us. We live on a beautiful planet, the more appreciation we have for that, the more we will care for it.

The additional benefit of being at-one with the Earth is that it supports manifestation. Every thing you manifest in the world is granted to you by the raw elemental particles of the Earth. Literally, every thing needs Earth's particles in order to present as matter in the physical world. So, as you develop your relationship with the energies of Earth, you actually become more skilled at attracting and manifesting in the material world.

As your power builds, your energy field will naturally expand and become more radiant. You will then be living less 'contained' and come into an open state of flow. The less 'contained' your energy field, the more you will be able to magnetise and attract into your life that which you desire.

I mentioned previously how you connect into multiple time zones and places, which has the potential to disperse your energy if you do not manage awareness of your activity. The benefit of being stable in the ground, with more power in your energy field, means your power of magnetism is greater. Therefore when you make an outward energetic connection your energy resources will naturally return to you and not remain elsewhere in time or space. The power within your energy field will naturally re-attract and recall your own personal energies as they move fluidly in and out of different situations and circumstances. Your ability to remain whole and stable then increases considerably and you will almost completely eliminate stress and energy conflict from your life.

Imagine that, moving effortlessly through all your life transactions, activities and tasks throughout each day - knowing that your energy is so strong and stable it will naturally and automatically re-stabilise itself. As you become more powerful, with greater management skills and awareness, your capacity for life transactions will naturally increase - you can 'do' more.

Let's recap on the Four Elements to stable and powerful energy:

- Clear yourself of all energetic debris by applying with intent the command to Disconnect (Chapter 7)
- Reclaim your personal energies to your core centre by applying the Reclaim command (Chapter 9)
- Work to develop a good, strong and stable ground connection (this Chapter)
- With your intent, command yourself fully into the NOW moment.

These are the basics to managing your personal energy on a regular basis. The benefits from these four elements alone will be immediately noticeable. They will change the way you feel, the clarity of your thinking and the level of empowered choices you make within your life.

If you combine daily energy management with a commitment to heal your wounds and clear your past patterns, your scope and quality of living will surpass your imaginations.

Please bear in mind that if you become stressed, anxious or fearful, you will naturally withdraw your energy up from the ground. These emotional states cause you to limit your energetic flows and connections and return you to the 'contained' state I mentioned very early on in this book. As such, the energy field becomes smaller and withdraws upwards from any depth of connection it had with the ground. The immediate effect of returning to the 'contained' state is less energy resource, less stability and less strength. Such a state will then limit your creativity and true expression in the world.

If such circumstances occur, your priority should be to deal with the feelings and energy forms that have caused such a non-serving state. Once they are cleared, recommence working towards cultivating a good strong ground connection.

Throughout my time of teaching, I have trained many for whom it is critical they find better and stronger ways to remain energetically stable because their work requires it. These include healers, therapists, 'readers', mediums and psychics who may have possessed very little energy knowledge, but are still required to work responsibly with higher energies in their service to others.

I have come to know the one fundamental that everyone has to understand - if you wish to commune more with higher energies in order to live in accord with your higher potentials and core values, then you need a stable grounding. Strength and ability 'up there' in higher consciousness, comes by way of strength and connection 'down here' with the Earth. The development and maintenance of the balance between those two aspects is absolutely vital.

The more depth and stability in the grounding, the more you can expand your energies into higher awareness. Who doesn't want to live their soul? Surely, we all seek to connect to that higher place of love and grace that brings joy and happiness to life. Basically, if you want to get 'up there' to those higher frequency energies that enlighten - then you need to be stable 'down here', rooted well into the Earth. That's the only balanced way to achieve wholeness. It is the only balanced way to achieve an expansive consciousness.

Whilst my first claim would always be that practical energy management is life management, we also need to understand more fully what we are working with. This energy field is your field of consciousness. Therefore, changes and transformation made to energy flows, alters the flow of consciousness. Development in consciousness is spiritual development. Therefore, subtle energy awareness affords us opportunity for the spiritual essence of life to be a fully integrated part of daily life. As we come to understand that all things are energy, then ultimately we see that all things are spirit. Every thought, feeling, action and deed is a daily spiritual activity. Doesn't this offer us a new perspective through which to view the quality, content and meaning of our lives?

"Having received healing from Sue, after which I always felt so calm, clear headed, extremely light and 'feeling I could do anything', my interest in the realm of subtle energy and how it could help me in my life as a whole was ignited. I studied Energy Field Healing with Sue, and the teaching programmes, all of which followed on beautifully from one another, increasing my learning and growth in this field.

Sue's skill in purveying her knowledge to teach us how to manage and keep clear our own energy field has helped me on a daily basis to be calmer, more focused, more positive and more aware. I have developed awareness of others' energy, of my family dynamic, and how the current energetic state tells a story and explains why we say and act as we do. But the beauty of energy awareness is that by clearing up the denseness and bringing in the light, we can create new potential.

Being 'energy aware' has opened up my creativity, an area in which I felt stuck for ages, wanting to move forward but not knowing how or why I couldn't. I now feel and know that I am going forward. I have found only positive benefits from discovering this invisible world of subtle energy, and the simple exercises taught by Sue, are a great starting point for anyone wanting to grow spiritually or to simply become more balanced. I look at the World through different eyes now, and there is no going back – it is what it is!"

L. Goodwin, Finance Director &
Certified Inspirit Teacher

Let's Get Spiritual | 11

"Make your endeavours worthy of the highest beauty of your soul."

The two most profound effects of maintaining stable energy flow are a greater capacity to engage in life and the transformation brought by the raising of energy resonance. The higher resonances of energy are fine, beautiful and fully engaged with your true heart's desires.

A stable and clear energy will ensure you have all of the frequencies of energy required for your well-being flowing throughout your field and within your body. You will be absorbing the necessary sustenance of the ground energies and, the incoming higher cosmic energies will lighten your presence.

As the higher frequencies of energy establish in your field, you become more open to the higher frequency emotions - joy, love, kinship, generosity, kindness, compassion and forgiveness. Your views and perspectives of life will change - you will see the World through different eyes.

Most especially, the presence of these higher energies will activate the core values you hold deep within you. You will become more true to yourself. Your heart will open and reveal its true desires and your capacity for love (the true inner being you are) will flow into the World on a daily basis.

If we understand energy as consciousness, and consciousness as spirit, we will develop a way to make our choices better, our days more enjoyable and our outcomes, long and short term, will be what we truly desire for our lives.

The raising of your awareness is an evolutionary process - the evolution of your consciousness. As you learn to manage and command the flows of your consciousness (energy), you will naturally come to live in alignment and accord with this new enlightened awareness.

Become an enhanced field of consciousness

In Picture 8 (opposite) you can see how the depth of good grounding has created a greater capacity within the energy field. This field is over a metre in radius from the body, it is stable, it has great presence and it is strong. The vibrant emotions and feelings flowing through this field keep it buoyant and light. Such a field is open and ready to engage in the beauty of life and the next wonderful offering of the day.

This is an enhanced energy field, which naturally has greater potential and capacity. The ability of the enhanced field to magnetise and attract what it truly desires in life is far greater. It is capable of managing and handling multiple energy transactions throughout the day.

Such a state is a spiritual enhancement and one of the most important advantages of this is the ability to 'see the bigger picture'. An enhanced field of consciousness gives you the ability to connect with more views, higher perspectives, more options and solutions. In a nutshell - it brings inspiration and wisdom!

As the mind energies expand we connect into higher intelligence. It's a state of expanded consciousness where the mind, higher mind, and spiritual intelligence, combine. It offers more meaningful insight to life, to your presence in the World and to creation.

This enhanced state of consciousness can analyse, process and sequence the flow of mental transactions at great speed, whilst aligning such with the motives and desires of the heart energy. This synergy between thought and feeling

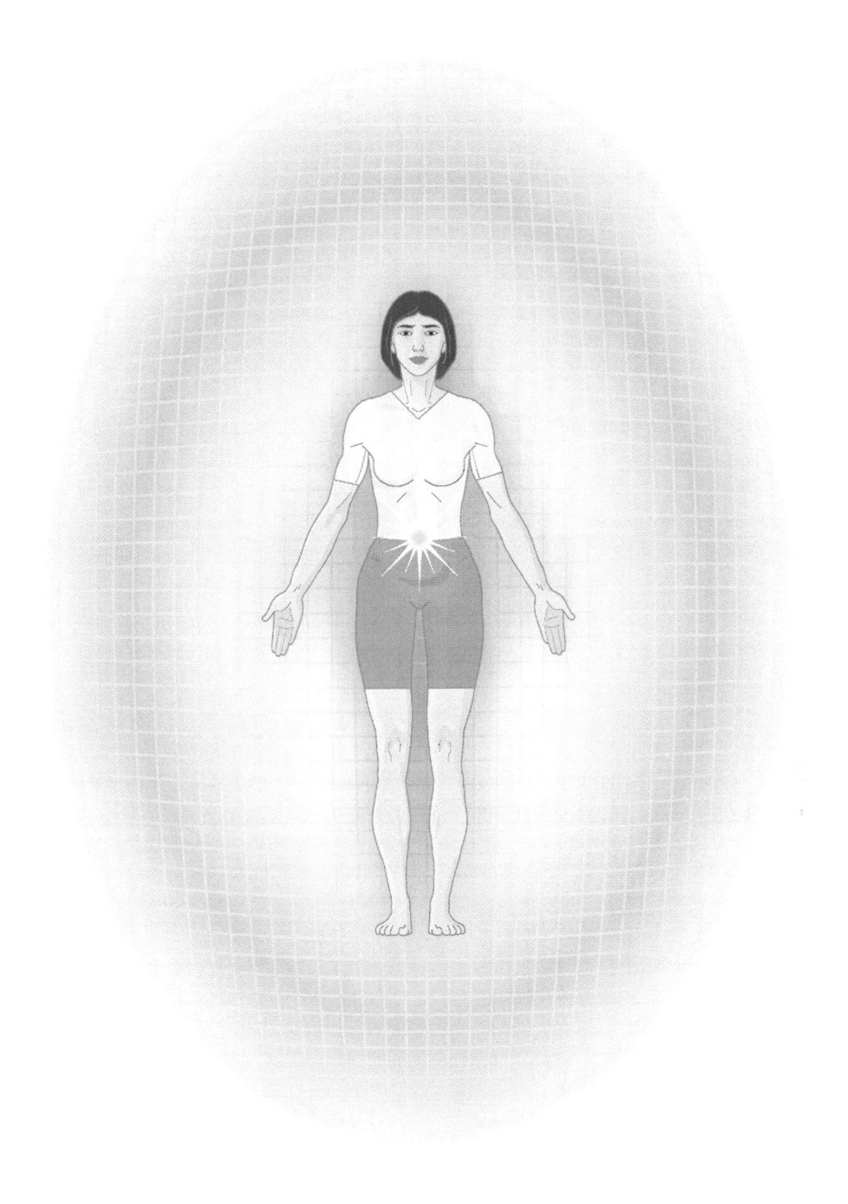

Picture 8 - Expansive, Balanced, Open & Lovingly Engaged Energy Field

creates an inner and outer wholeness. It is a state whereby the mind becomes of service to the heart.

Let's talk a little more about higher intelligence, because until you have experienced the flow of this, it may not mean anything to you. Our life transactions continuously present the need for solutions, options, ideas, innovation, resolution and furtherance. In a 'contained' state of energy flow, these aspects are limited and so is the ability to gain greater access to them. It isn't that the solutions or options are not there, it's just that we cannot see them, or bring them to mind.

When the energy is in an expanded state it can access those higher intelligent functions with ease. It is a little like putting all the options and potential solutions spread out on a large table, where you can clearly see and consider them. In this state, you can sort things correctly and position them into rightful order and priority. Through analysis, you can make choices and decisions as to the most serving option or solution. Most especially, because all the options are clear, you remove yourself from doubt, second-guessing and the insecurity of wondering or indecision. Clear directive focus is the product of expansive mental energies - higher intelligence.

Higher intelligence is an enhanced function

How much time would you save each day if you could be clear and accurate in your decisions? How much distress would be eliminated if you didn't fret over multiple 'what if's'? If you could process and decisively act with speed and precision - how much more could you achieve each day? How much more could you achieve in your life? When we see with the vision of higher intelligence, we function in an enhanced state.

Let's consider ideas and inspiration. It is common practise for people to wait for inspiration, to wait for an idea to come, to wait to see if a solution is possible! You will often hear people say "Oh, I'll sleep on it", or "I have no idea what to do about it". And people just wait, completely unaware that they could pro-actively seek that inspiration by way of commanding their own higher awareness.

During the early 1990's I was working in business management. I had a fairly pressurised job, but a lot of natural ability that tended to keep me 'on the ball'. At that time, I would have said outright "I'm not an ideas person". I would wait for others in the team to come up with an idea or option and quite effectively, I could put it straight into operation. I was a 'do-er'.

Back then, it was the heyday of business development gurus and in management we were being trained on how to develop groups with a specific member for each of the key roles and functions, based on each of their own practical aptitudes. (Makes me smile to think about it now and how limited a view it was... is!) However, that was the theme of the decade and masses of financial and time resources were committed by organisations Worldwide to enhance the productivity of their workforce by developing these team roles within defined criteria.

When life circumstances changed for me in 1997 and illness led me onto an unusual development path of spiritual growth and energy awareness, my life took an enormous leap in evolution. As the higher energies of a raised awareness became a consistent part of my every-day presence, I discovered that ideas and inspiration are a natural and continuous function of the higher intelligence within consciousness.

Creative ideas just kept pouring into me, every day. I had become an 'ideas person'! Any daily challenge or problem was no longer so, I could quickly direct my mind to options and there they would be. After so many years of practising enhanced awareness, I live each day with more ideas and inspiration than I can put into action. Solutions to any situation or challenge just flow straight into my awareness. All I need do is direct my focus to the subtle energy nature of the situation and its potentials are clearly there to be seen and considered.

I have made this part of my primary service now to clients, because I am a physical conduit for higher consciousness awareness. I apply my skills to be their solution finder, their builder of higher potentials, their inspirational resource. By applying subtle energy techniques, it is possible to construct an infrastructure of co-operation and unified contribution that engages and enriches everyone. This method enables everyone involved to offer their highest potential to any aspect of the work - inspiration, creation, productivity, task completion, development, management and ultimately, the highest serving outcome.

Working with the subtle energy infrastructure within a group ensures every ounce of collaborative goodwill becomes engaged with a project. A team operating within such an enhanced intelligent dynamic doesn't just settle for getting a little of the good from each member. It becomes capable of far greater unified potential and creativity. A divine flow of synergy - where the combined aspects exceed the sum of all the individual elements.

The subtle energy infrastructure of any situation or circumstance can be 'read', interpreted and enhanced. Blocks and hindrances can be cleared and new potentials opened. I do this for businesses, organisations, entrepreneurs and leaders, and even some high profile individuals. So, if it can be done powerfully and effectively on a group scale, I can assure you that you are capable of effecting change for yourself, as an individual within your own life.

I want to highlight to you the fact that I moved within a very short time, from believing I wasn't an 'ideas person', to someone who has an abundance of ideas and creative solutions just overflowing into daily life. It shows that it's possible

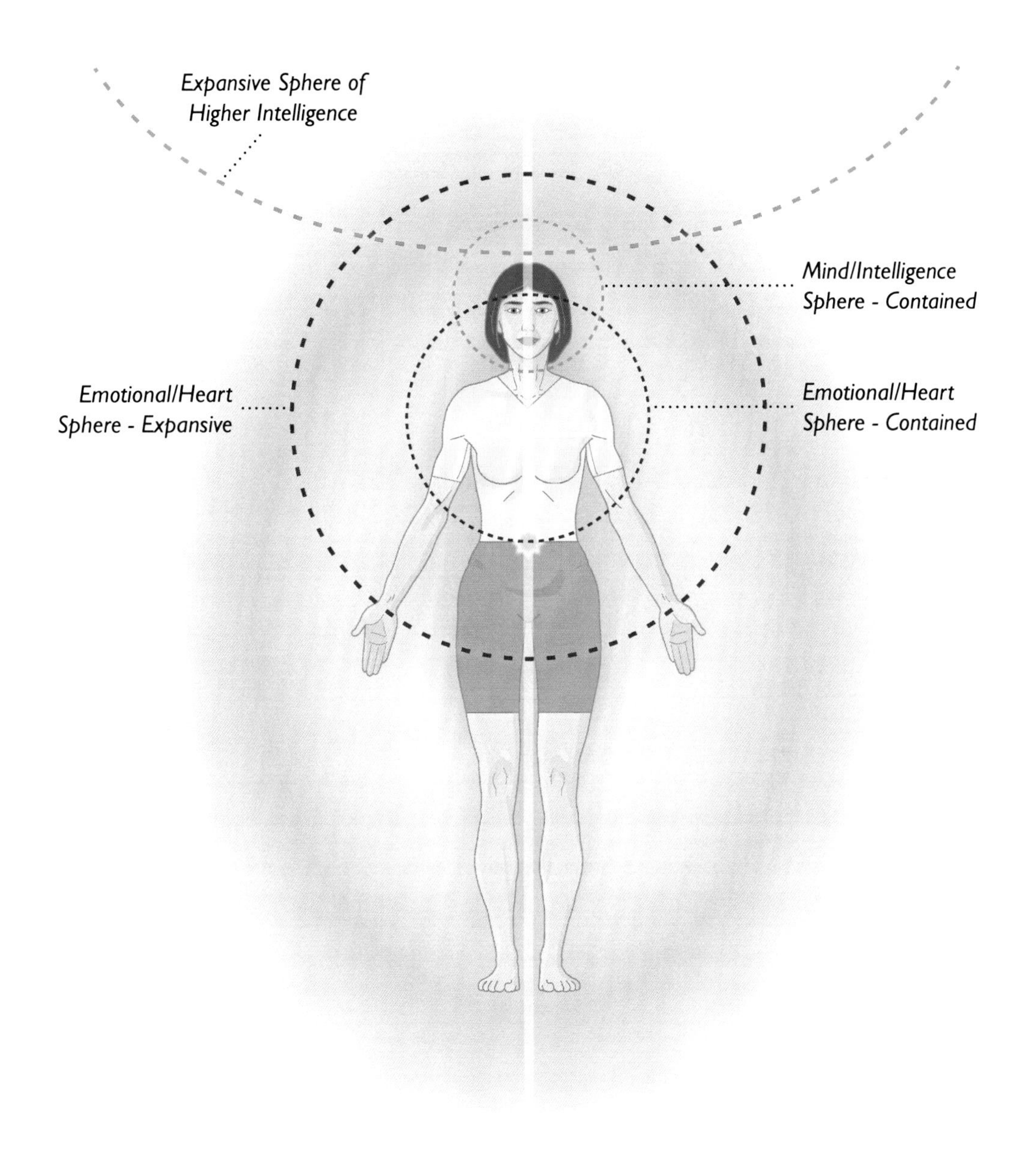

Picture 9 - Expanded Heart Energy engages Expansive Intelligence

and if you adopt the easily applied techniques within this book, your greater potential for empowerment and change will open. You just need to understand the energy mechanics of how these aspects of life flow. Please take a look at Picture 9 (previous page), to understand how a clear, vibrant and balanced energy becomes 'expansive'.

Higher intelligence occurs when we expand our field of consciousness (the energy field). Consider what you now know of the 'contained' energy field and relate these to the 'Emotional Sphere' and 'Mind Sphere' shown in Picture 9. You can see from the diagram that the spheres of activity and their capacity are minimal when in the 'contained' state.

Once the heart is open and the energy field expanded, the scope and potential is exponentially increased. The open flow of heart energy naturally raises the mind and intelligence functions. The 'Expansive Sphere of Intelligence' connects into higher realms of consciousness, where great things become possible. Higher realms of intelligence offer vast potentials for creativity and innovation. Combined with the loving energies of an open and high vibrational 'Emotional Sphere', all things may become serving.

Cultivate those higher feelings of love, kindness, compassion and joy

The first steps to expanding the energy field have already been given to you in previous chapters. A strong, clear and balanced energy field is a powerful energy field. That power can be directed by your command and maintained by those higher frequencies of energy - love.

Inspiration flows from the heart - it is not a mental activity. It is a state of grace which flows through us as a product of living in accord with our own love, beauty and heartfelt desires. True inspiration will always be in alignment with your core inner purpose and values.

To be inspired, is to be in love. An enhanced, clear energy field is abundant with the flow of those higher resonance feelings and emotions. There's a glorious bonus to being in love with your life - the 'inner you' emerges into the outer World. All the beauty and potential you hold for life deep within you, will start flowing out into everything you do on a daily basis. And it will show. People will comment on it and, people will want to be in its presence. Love is very attractive.

With an open field, you will find it very easy to love, easy to be kind, easy to enact compassion, easy to forgive. This natural state of expansion has occurred for me and has enlightened my journey through life. I have witnessed this development in others that I have supported in healing, trained and mentored. If I can imprint one seed upon your consciousness right now, it would be that your spiritual journey is one of love, towards love, because of love, for the generation and expression of love. No aspect of life can sustain without it. It is wise to be unafraid of the greater glory of the spirit within you.

Once the loving heart is engaged in living, life starts to be in service to its highest potential. The inflow of higher frequency energies will transform every aspect of your life.

The development of an enhanced field of consciousness can offer you a quality of life that is beyond what you can think, or imagine possible. It will offer you a vision of infinite potential and the confidence to put that into action. It will open your heart to the light of the greatness within you and gently, and most certainly, bring you into alignment with your destiny.

It will also bring to you a daily peace and contentment, clear focus, purpose and meaning. The greater potentials and opportunities that arrive will serve to offer you a higher quality life where value, service and kinship flow naturally from within you, out to every one and every circumstance.

Such spiritual development brings you to the place of inter-connectedness. The place where you discover that all things are one. That we, as the group of humanity, are all held within a unified field of consciousness and that we are together. You will discover that we are each unique and individualised aspects of the same. That we originate from and return to this vast expanse of unified consciousness and that therefore, we have the time in this lifetime, to make our own unique contribution. To gift the world, to share, to enrich, to love, and to leave the physical World a little better and richer than it was before our arrival.

Our inter-connectedness within this unified field of consciousness ensures our togetherness, it anchors our commonalities, and compels us to contribute to the greater good. We only become whole as an individual, when we recognise and validate the wholeness of all. That we are one, that we have the capacity to be in love with each other, and that our primary and foremost fundamental law of connection must surely be 'first, cause no harm'.

The pursuance of your day to day energy awareness and techniques will lead you to a greater place. It is my desire that you discover the practical elements of energy awareness that will enrich your life on a daily basis, so that you can live practically and more well by applying this knowledge.

Ultimately, your journey will bring you to the higher principles of understanding the spiritual nature of your Being. It is inevitable, for you cannot know energy without raising your vibration. You cannot raise your vibration without feeling greater love. And the experience of greater love recognises the beauty, wholeness and splendour of the unified field of consciousness.

Peace, Calm and Wholeness | 12

"Life isn't about finding those magical few moments when you feel deep and enriching love. It's about maintaining a lifestyle that makes such love continuously possible each and every day."

As you achieve a greater capacity within your energy, whereby you are now attaining an enhanced state of being, your higher awareness will need maintenance!

An enhanced state of consciousness requires you to remain aware. Most especially, aware of all and any aspects of life that may attempt to limit or lessen that enhanced state. As with all powerful life transitions, you need to be able to maintain and sustain such development.

When I trained my healing students, I equipped them with an 'Energy Toolbox'. The knowledge of the skills and techniques to work with energy, healing and transformation, is placed in the energy toolbox and therefore positioned in consciousness. At any time then, they can easily access the toolbox and call to their command the skill or technique they require.

Subtle energy awareness needs to be continually developed to be in accord with your life growth. It isn't something you just learn about or 'do', it's a way of life. Every contribution you make in time or resources to maintaining your enhanced state of being, is an investment in the higher quality of your life and of every creative act you pursue.

The 5 primary elements to maintaining an enhanced state of Being:

1. The ability to be still.
2. Learning to identify and manage chaos and non-serving energies.
3. Concluding your daily transactions fully.
4. Commencing your daily transactions with directive intent.
5. Taking regular time for good quality visualisation and meditation.

Stillness

In previous chapters you have learned about the busy nature of incoming and outgoing energy transactions. No matter what level of saturation you are at, you must learn to become still.

When I say be still, I mean your body, your mind and your emotions. You need to learn this such that it can be your nature at any moment, in any given situation, no matter what is going on around you. It is also a vital component of energy management when you are connecting to other people.

Imagine entering a room full of people for a social occasion. You are engaging with an energy dynamic of which you are not in command. This dynamic is 'owned' by the group energy. So by the time you arrive, a certain resonance of energy will be holding the group together. You have to come into accord with that energetically in order to become part of the group, to become social. Have you never wondered why some people are more comfortable arriving early or first at an event? What about those who prefer to enter much later? It's an unconscious choice which is derived from the subtle energy senses that people can manage - their ease or unease within the group dynamic. Those that arrive early get to start the build of the dynamic, those that arrive later have to fit into it, or remain exempt.

As you enter the group environment, your own energy will begin to absorb the energies generated and transmitted by the group. Think about that for a moment. By joining a group, you will engage with their energies, everything being transmitted by each member into the group dynamic.

Now if you've understood fully what I have been explaining, you will now realise that entering into a group means you will become influenced by their thinking, will align to their emotional content, in order to 'be with them'. That, is what peer pressure is - it's the subtle energy presence that commands you conform. The only way you will not adapt to the essence of a group dynamic is if you are able to maintain your own individual integrity of presence whilst within that dynamic. Such integrity of presence requires your understanding and attention to your own inner core power and strength.

If you enter a group environment when your energy is chaotic, over-busy, or weak in flow, you are more vulnerable to group influence. You are also more at risk of your emotions being triggered because groups come together as a 'tribe' on an emotional level. What's the first thing you ask people when you enter a group... "How are you?" Groups connect to each other by opening up the emotional content of the subtle energies in the field. From there, each person calculates the power level, the attraction, the intent, the likeability and potential value of each member. This is a function that takes place in subtle energy, though usually without conscious awareness of most of the group members.

A still and calm energy will be able to align to the resonance of the dynamic it needs to join. A still energy, is an alert energy, it will be able to sense the tone and nature of the group gathering and adapt accordingly, whilst maintaining its own strength and purpose. As the strong energy 'reads' the tone of the dynamic of the group, such a person will be aware and intelligently responsive. The strongest, most aware energy within the group becomes the one in command.

I am outlining for you the means by which you can powerfully, commandingly and, with presence, enter into any situation. If you commence from a place of inner stillness, then you are in command of your response to everything that transpires around you. Your awareness will ensure you contribute effectively and positively to the group's purpose. You will also limit the degree of any non-serving influence from the subtle energy transactions flowing within the group dynamic, which can affect you on both a mental and emotional level. Stillness initiates intelligent awareness.

I don't think I can make it too clear that energy management and therefore, command of your life, depends on your ability to be still. It may sound simple, but our modern world is not set up for stillness. Practise being still until you have it to a fine art.

The 6 quick energy skills for stillness:

- Stop all activity.
- State the Disconnection Command.
- Visualise connection to ground and discharge energy 'debris'.
- State the Reclaim Command.
- Call your energy into time - the 'Now' moment.
- Physically, remain still and wait a few moments.

When you first attempt stillness you will find it takes a short while for your body to settle. You may have to take time to calm your emotions and then await the backlog of your mind processing. The process can take 10-15 minutes whilst you are learning. However, with regular practise, you will be able to come to stillness by command, within seconds.

When carrying out an energy field healing, the healer has to learn how to engage their own energy field with the client's energy field, in order to 'read' the energy state and detect anything that needs clearing or transforming. To achieve that communion in energy, the healer has to smoothly correspond with the resonance of the client's field. To facilitate that, the healer starts first from the most powerful place, stillness. It's one of the early skills placed in the 'energy toolbox'.

Your energy is a field of intelligence, it will learn very quickly what you want to achieve as it becomes familiar with the intent of your commands. So each and every time you do the stillness exercise, your intelligence will adopt the procedure more quickly. At some stage, the process will become an automatic energy function - by command and within seconds, you will become still.

Use stillness to manage chaos and non-serving energies

The signs of chaos and non-serving energy should now be more noticeable to you - those times when you are 'all over the place'. You may be dropping things, bumping into things, running late, feeling unstable or wobbly, unable to think clearly, or full of emotions that feel like they are about to erupt out of you. Enacting stillness at these times will transform your ability to manage and redirect.

When energies are balanced and flowing correctly, we are accurate and defined in our movements and actions. We detect direction, locality and proximity with our subtle energy senses and respond accordingly. When our energy is overloaded or imbalanced our natural sensory functions do not operate correctly. The next time you are 'out of sorts' and 'off the ball' you need to understand that your energetic condition is revealing itself.

Already in your 'energy toolbox' you have the Disconnection and Reclaiming Commands. So incorporate them into a stillness exercise and use them. Do not accept a lower standard or quality of living now that you are empowered to take action to make it otherwise.

If you are feeling low or depressed without any explanation, then consider the amount of emotional energy debris you may have absorbed from others. Your feelings are dramatically affected when you absorb others' low or dense energies. I shall explain some more about connections to other people and the energies of relationships in the following chapter.

Conclude your daily transactions fully

As the night draws near, is your mind still mulling over the day's events? Are you still feeling the stress of being overloaded with tasks? Or are you distracted by what remains to be done rather than being able to relax, socialise and enjoy your free time? Do you find yourself going to bed with random thoughts and tasks still consuming you, or perhaps distressed feelings you haven't been able to discharge or resolve?

How you conclude and fulfil your day's activity will dictate how you commence the next one. More importantly though, what you take into sleep with you will dictate the quality of that night's rest.

If you desire to manage your life in an empowered and creative manner, you cannot live with restless nights, lack of sleep and limited restoration of the body. This state cannot be maintained for any length of time and you should consider this unacceptable.

The best energy technique available is to move the energy forms of what is still buzzing through your mind, into a physical form. Yes, it's as simple as that - write down on a pad what you are still thinking about. The act of changing an energy process into a physical actuality changes its presence in your field, because you have enacted it. You have directed the energy charge elsewhere. By writing it down, it becomes created in the physical, you will have removed the energy form from your field.

This is a really simple positioning technique that doesn't require you to hold anything further in energy form. It will clear your mind, until you are ready to re-engage with it the following day.

Be aware that when you are busy your brain processes transactions at a backlog. The brain is continually sequencing all your thoughts in line with priorities, focus and non-focus. Once you stop all activity, it may require you to be still for a few minutes without allowing any further data to be input, in order to calm the mental activity. Your brain needs the opportunity to clear its processing so you gain a clear space to focus on positioning any thoughts or ideas that are needed for the following day. Once those thoughts are written down, you can let them go. Your higher intelligence will re-schedule them in line with your intentions during the next day and of course, you now have the written reminder.

If the energy activity that is keeping you from sleep is emotional and feeling based, rather than mental busy-ness, then I offer you an excellent and simple visualisation exercise for this just a little later in this chapter. As you are now aware, emotional energies are very different from mental energies and, therefore, we deal with them differently.

Remember, energy management is life management. One of the key elements of managing energies is to create calm, balance and clarity. You need all three of these aspects to enjoy a peaceful and quality night of sleep. One of the fundamentals to fulfilling a day properly is clearance and management of the daily energy transactions. You have in your 'energy toolbox' the Disconnection and Reclaim Commands. These should be applied before settling in the evening.

As a healer I saw far too many scenarios of people with ill-health caused by an inability to manage stressful energy transactions and/or restore through their night's sleep. As I have explained, everyone has capacity and when we exceed that, we become vulnerable to energy breakdown. If extended longer term, this can create serious states of ill-health and emotional and mental dysfunction. Sleep, good quality sleep, is designed to be your physical, emotional and mental re-balancer. It is essential, not optional.

Unfortunately, when the subtle energy system becomes disrupted, overloaded, or enters a state of breakdown, it is sleep that suffers. So the body and energy system no longer have the opportunity to repair and restore.

Sleep and good rest are absolutely vital. We engage in mass processing of energy data whilst we sleep. Poor sleeping will result in rapid build up of energy overload, imbalance and a stagnant flowing system. One of the key specialisms of energy field healing is the re-balancing of energy flows and the rebuilding of the structure of the field. I have cared for people in all walks of life who have gone beyond the state of self-ability to restore - people who exceed their capacity and then experience the resulting energetic dysfunction. Many of those clients have not called upon my services until they are in complete breakdown!

I am the person that gets called in when things are failing on all levels, because my energy skills allow me to clear, transform and rebuild the fundamental energy structure. It is best not to get to that state. Burn-out is a product of over-capacity and mismanagement of energy transactions. Breakdown is a product of ignoring the burn-out.

These scenarios exist for anyone, from high level business people with over-burden of responsibilities, right through to working mothers who are dealing with too many tasks and becoming fraught with family commitments and work stress. As my clients have discovered, these energetic situations can be resolved by applying specialised energy field healing techniques.

I have educated all my clients to understand that if they apply energy management tools regularly and add the occasional skills of an energy field healer to their maintenance programme, they can manage their activity and workload with greater ease. They become more productive, more inspired, more aware of the needs of others. Their directive thinking and ability to create becomes greatly enhanced. The additional benefits of course are the increased quality and value created for their personal and family living.

Let's be clear about this. You should not be going to bed with a mind full of 'happenings', emotions churned up with unsettled feelings, or tension and stress within your body. That is not a reasonable way to live. Make a better choice.

So, to ensure you are not living with a continual build up of dysfunction in the energy system, how you conclude and fulfil your daily transactions is essential management.

If you find yourself emotionally distressed at night, then it is likely that you have encountered emotional energies during the day which have triggered something within your own deeper issues. When a deeper wound or issue is triggered, it is often covered up by daily busy-ness and not given the attention it requires. Let me give you another technique for your Energy Toolbox:

Exercise to clear unsettled feelings:

1. Be still and quiet. Breathe and try to relax a little.
2. Ask yourself "What's the feeling that's on the surface?". Then wait until you identify and can name that feeling.
3. Then ask yourself "What's the underlying feeling?". This will take your enquiry deeper. Our default is often to hide the emotional truth. By probing more deeply, you will find the core feeling that needs attention.

4. Then ask "When is the LAST time I felt this?". And wait. In your mind's eye, you will get an image of the last time you felt that feeling. It will open the visual imagery for you, perhaps showing the people involved or the event. Now you have some basic information.
5. Then ask "When is the FIRST time I felt like this?". This question activates your higher intelligence and a line of enquiry will ensue. Working from the LAST time that emotion was felt, the energy lines will open and start moving through layers of experience. Ultimately, the original wound/issue will be found - the FIRST time occurrence. Again, your mind's eye will open up the 'visual' for you and you will be able to see what actually happened.
6. At this stage - make a choice to heal the point of origin of those feelings. Recall our three steps to the healing process - acceptance, forgiveness, and love. If you can choose to offer those up in your own grace, you will transform the energies of the original scenario. If you have been developing your visualisation skills, then you may visualise golden rays of healing energy coming into that scenario, and it will transform.
7. In consciousness, you have moved back in time for this exercise. Once you feel the issue has changed and is releasing, it is important to return your awareness fully to the 'now moment'. Do this through your intention - "I reclaim my energies fully into the Now moment".

Whilst you are learning this technique, it may take you 15-20 minutes to enact. Once you train your higher intelligence in this function, you will discover that the whole process can be achieved in 5 minutes or less.

It is highly effective. I have been teaching this to my students for many years as a way by which they can deal with issues as they arise, rather than carry them for periods of time, which may generate greater emotional impact.

It is a very simple process - identify the feeling, follow through to the last time it occurred. Then take it further to the first time it occurred. Apply healing light (gold is very easy to visualise). Return your awareness to the 'now'. The exercise will become very familiar to you as you regularly employ it and you will discover it is easy and effective at making change for you.

By this stage I am sure you are becoming more aware of the state of your being. You will realise that there will be issues and wounds that you can deal with yourself. There will also be times when you need the assistance of a professional to support you through transformation. Make a choice that serves you well and which you know you can manage.

On a final note about concluding your day - be grateful. Whatever the day has brought, it will have had richness within it. Layered within the fineness of life activity, there is always a spiritual richness that helps us to grow and enhance our lives. Take a few moments to feel content with your achievements that day, big or small. Reflect upon the goodness, kindness and fun that you shared with others. Take some moments to value the process of that day and be grateful for the life experience it has brought.

Commence your daily transactions with clear direction

Wake up a few minutes earlier! I can't over stress the benefits of taking just a few minutes in the morning to position the flow of your day. To do that, you need just a few extra minutes before the day's physical activities commence.

Most people hear the alarm, slide out of bed, head in the general direction of the bathroom, then take about 20 minutes to get their mind focused and working. The majority of people will just function on auto-pilot and auto-ritual in order to get to the point where they believe the day fully begins. For some, that may be breakfast with the family, or the school run, or even the arrival at the office.

If you start your day on 'default' it will likely run its entire course aligned to the energy movements, needs and intentions of others and you will struggle to get command of your time and actions. That is not an empowered way to live.

First things first - when you wake in the morning, do the Reclaim Command. During the sleep state we process an immense amount of life content. Through our dreams and through an expanded state created by sleep, a great many transactions take place. That process scatters energies into different places, times and connections to others. So, do the Reclaim Command and get your energy fully to Core Centre before you even move out of the bed.

Secondly, assess your view of the day that is about to be presented to you. This day is a gift through which you can enjoy, grow, learn, be of service and create. Each and every day is both a privilege and a blessing, so surely it makes sense to make the most of its potential.

Every day we all have certain tasks to fulfil. We may have projects and meetings, chores and calls. You will have your own view about how you value all of that and what it means to you. Within the interweave of all those functions, the day will also hold moments of glorious potential for you. This is potential for joy, for kinship, for fun, for creative expression, for happiness. For this very reason, it makes good sense to be grateful in advance! Grateful for all the potential that the day may bring.

So, as you awaken and after reclaiming your energies, position how you feel about the day to come and be grateful for its blessings. If your outlook for the forthcoming day is positive and serving, then your transactions will follow your directive intent.

If you genuinely wake up and are dismayed by the prospects of the day to come, then you need to make different choices for your lifestyle and what you are involved in. Your life is precious, live it so. Make the changes you need to make so that you can enjoy the prospect of any new day.

So again, before you move out of the bed - position your key intentions for the day and map an outline in your mind of how the day may flow. This gives the day directive focus and puts the energy intent into the key objectives you need to achieve. All other transactions then will move fluidly around the core of that intent and will not distract or consume you.

For example, a typical morning waking for me would perhaps commence with positioning my focus on the key aspects or priorities of the day - "I'll write the blog post about so-n-so, I have the session this afternoon with client x-y, dinner with friends this evening, and I need to start designing the itinerary for the new development course". So, I have four primary matters that need my attention that day. By bringing them to focus, I have positioned them in space, maybe time, but certainly I will have built a core energy intent for them. Around that core, I will have the minor matters occurring, but so long as I hold my core intent, I know I am directing the day towards achievement and progress.

Now I'm also human, I have others around me who have needs and so 'stuff' will happen. It is possible that sometimes plans will change and move, interruptions will occur and occasionally, a crisis may need my attention. I am on-call for the majority of my business clients, so every day has to remain fluid and adaptable. However the great thing about holding a core intent, is that it can easily be repositioned in energy flows because it is held in command. This process keeps me fluid and responsive to change in circumstances.

An outline energy map for the day is essential if you desire to be empowered to enact that day on your terms and in line with your choices. If you have no directive purpose for your day, I can assure you that others will consume it, or it will be wasted and you may be living reactively. It is most dissatisfying to get to the end of a day and feel no sense of joy, achievement or progress. Time is the most valuable commodity for all of us, don't let it be wasted by a lack of directive intent on your part.

This principle does not just apply to work days or busy days. You can also position your energy intent for rest days, where relaxation and enjoyment of hobbies are the aspects that build your core intent.

So, set five minutes earlier on the alarm clock - reclaim your energies, outline your day, and then get out of that bed with purpose!

The ultimate objective - Peace of Mind

I believe every single one of us would agree that peace of mind is important. That's because we all, at some time or other, lose our peace of mind. It is those times when it is lost, that we come to understand just how important it is.

A troubled mind is destructive to our creativity. It entangles us in complexity and exaggeration that propels us into nonsense. We become unreasonable when we cannot quieten our mind, because we are living with the continual feeling that things are going out of control. Underneath all that, our fears are sparking off and moving us into annoyance, frustration and anger.

A peaceful mind can luxuriate in the domain of wisdom, enriching daily activities with inspiration, directive thinking and meaningful purpose. I hope that by this stage in the book, you have come to realise that an over-busy energy system is the leading factor that affects your state of mind.

When you consider just how easy it is to begin to clear the over active and potentially chaotic energies, then it makes great sense to apply such simple techniques. I consider we have too many occasions of disempowered states in this World. Too many days of not thinking for ourselves. Too many occasions of not choosing wisely or with awareness.

It is our choices that carve out the creation of our lives. Surely we owe it to ourselves and to all those whose lives we affect, to make choices that benefit, enrich and serve well. That is such an easy conclusion to arrive at and yet, so many do not understand the influences that affect, change, alter or interfere with the choice making process.

You will have a different level of awareness upon you now, since you have learned some insight into how subtle energies are present and how they affect the natural processing functions of the mind, emotions and body. Your journey to wholeness, towards peace, is now finding its way.

"I was introduced to Energy Field Healing at a difficult time in my life. My marriage had ended, I was unhappy at work and I felt under a lot of pressure. The training and the healing I experienced enabled me to make sense of everything that happened to me in my life. As I became calmer and more understanding, my relationships with other people improved.

I have been able to see things from a different perspective, one that gives me a broader view of the World and my place within it. Regular meditation has helped me to see the World as a place of wonder, to realise that God is present in everyone and every thing. I have learnt to savour the simple things in life and to understand how tiny gestures of kindness can make a big difference.

Subtle energy awareness has helped open my eyes to what I was missing in my life. My journey isn't over, but I feel as if I've been given a handbook on life."

K. Ford, Communications Officer and Certified Teacher
of The 'Enhance your Light' Meditation Programme

Managing Energy Zones | 13

"Your personal energy exists within multiple dimensions of space and time. These life-zones are influencing every aspect of who you are."

I want you to imagine now that as you process all your daily life transactions, energetically you are moving through a series of energy zones. Technically, these zones are the state and resonance of different dimensional energies. I want you to move your understanding beyond you and your personal energy field. I mentioned previously about joining group dynamics. Your family are an example of a group dynamic you reside within. There are also energy spaces, locations that you reside in and move through. Spaces and more particularly, spaces where people are energetically connected, are your energy zones of operation.

We all have energy zones in which we operate. For example, you have space zones - your home, your workplace, social meeting places and so on. You have people zones - the family you live with inside your home, your extended family and their homes, your social friends and the places you gather, your work colleagues and the work locations. Also there are, interwoven within all those spaces, time zones - the now moment, later, earlier, today, yesterday, last month, next month, the future or the past.

You now understand that the busier you are, the more transactions exist. So too, the more energy zones you will be moving and flowing within. That means there are far more energy aspects to be managed. If you are balanced and centred, then you are in command and transactions flow with ease, purpose, and meaning. As such, you are unlikely to notice or be bothered by changes in location, dynamics, or people movements. However, if you are stressed, energetically unstable and imbalanced then changes and movements of places and people will become stressful. In that case, the transactions will flow through like a 'jagged' movement, with unease and difficulty and will likely 'put you on edge'. You are generally more at ease with familiar people and familiar places. On a subtle level, your system has already assessed and assimilated the data for these known elements.

Have you ever wondered why some people get anxious about going to new places, or meeting new groups of people? Every situation and person has to be energetically assessed in order to become 'known'. New people or places can be challenging on a subtle level. A less strong or vulnerable energy may be very uncomfortable dealing with changed energies or new experiences.

What about noticing the change in your work colleagues when you take them out of the work environment? You are putting those people you know, into a new energy environment (zone). The energy dynamic will change and behaviour and character changes. As people adjust their energies to the new 'zone' you will discover things you didn't know about them. That's the whole basis of company team building days out, to put the usual energies and dynamics into a completely different energy environment. The result should be a change in the way individuals see and assess each other. Behaviours change considerably in unfamiliar environments and it's not always with a positive outcome.

Each energy 'zone' serves a purpose in your life. Each zone has a tone and essence to its energy, based on the nature of its purpose and its previous flows. So your home feels very different from your office. In your 'home zone' are those you live with and you share certain times of the day or week with them. The feel and essence of the energies you share with those people in that zone, will be very different to that which is present in other zones. You will appreciate that the feel and essence of your office, with the people you share work time for example, is a very different energy zone. You will most likely sense the energies of various zones as 'atmosphere'.

In energy terms, you are moving in, out and through different dimensional energies throughout each day. I refer to them as energy zones. These zones are the vibrational energies of different people, places, timings and purpose.

When you enter a space (energy zone) your personal energies will be affected by the resonance of the vibrations that are present in that space. So yes, the 'atmosphere' of a place will affect you. In addition, the energies that you are radiating, will pour into the space. So you are having an effect on the space. Ever wondered why particularly important meetings or negotiations should be done on 'neutral' ground. It's because the energies of either party will be established in their own places and others entering will be influenced by it. Any transaction that has to be done with equality and freedom of expression, should be carried out in an energetically neutral zone.

When you have regular and consistent connection with people, an energy dynamic is created. Groups build fine subtle energy connections which create these dynamics. By way of this energy dynamic, you will contribute energies with your intent and influence the way others feel. Their energies will also affect the way you feel. This process is particularly poignant when you re-enter a long-established group situation (family, work team, or social friends). The invisible threads join the group together based upon the purpose they serve. Therefore there is a powerful exchange and movement of energies between members of a group by way of the 'dynamic threads' and this can affect the way each individual feels and thinks. The degree to which you are affected depends upon the strength and integrity of your own field. If your energy is weak or 'exposed' you will be more greatly influenced by the energies of those you connect with.

Particular life Zones change feelings and behaviour

Take a moment to reflect upon how you feel or behave, in different environments with different people. Do you have scenarios where you perhaps take on a slightly different persona or identity? Are there zones where your archetypal psychology changes, or you begin to enact a role and your behaviour changes? How different are you at work, to how you are at home? How different are you with friends compared to how you are with your family unit? The varied resonance of different environments makes subtle changes to your own energy.

Whether you realise it or not your personality, the way you feel or think and most importantly your responses, reactions or behaviours, are influenced by the energy zones you reside within and the dynamics that exist there. On a subtle energy level, people change you, places change you, group dynamics change you.

It is only when you achieve a deep centred, inner self-awareness that you can remain consistent to the inner truth and core values of your own presence. You are not then so greatly affected or influenced as you move in and out of energy zones and dynamics.

It is important to understand that at certain times, perhaps when you may be feeling low, unwell, or distressed, you become more vulnerable to the influence of the energy zones around you. Both people and places will have greater energetic impact on you at such times, so it is wise to consider who you see and where you go when you are in such states of vulnerability.

Just consider for a moment, where are the places that you visit or occupy in which you feel unsettled, uncomfortable, perhaps low or 'out of sorts'? Is there a particular place that makes you miserable? You sense the energies of a place as 'atmosphere' or 'vibes', but actually, they are energetic environments.

What are the people interactions you encounter where you come away feeling unsettled, incomplete, puzzled, confounded, unhappy? Is there one group, or one zone in particular that 'gets you down'?

What time period in your life do you generally try to avoid thinking or talking about because it makes you so uncomfortable? Is it childhood years, or that first marriage? Or maybe the few years you felt emotionally unwell or mentally ill, or perhaps some time in a particular job? What time zone of your life has been a difficult time such that when you connect to it, the way you feel or think becomes changed?

All these things are examples of subtle energy influence within energy zones.

It's important to understand that the energy within zones and dynamics remains consistent and ever-present. So you can leave a place (zone) but the next time you return to it, the same energies will affect you. Places retain their energy essence, unless someone purposely applies energy cleansing techniques to clear those vibrations away.

As an example, let's say things have got difficult at home. A key relationship is troubled and home has become a place of arguments and misunderstandings. You go off to work and after a short while, are feeling a bit better and less disturbed by home events. You get on with the day, returning home feeling stronger and determined to improve matters. Upon re-entering that 'home-zone', within a very short space of time, the same arguments or misunderstandings flare up. Nothing has changed.

That situation occurs because the zone has become the incubator for those issues and is energetically resonating with the energy forms. You could relocate for a week, or longer, but when you returned the same issues will be there. Energy resonance does not change until the issues are energetically transformed.

I have worked with hundreds of people with emotional or stress disorders who are directly absorbing the energies of a particular zone. As energy field healers, we are capable of transforming both the energies of people and place. Clearing and transforming the energies of a home can have astounding results for the occupants in the way they feel, connect with each other and build potentials for the future.

In business, one of the last things management will think about is the energy of the workplace affecting their employees. There's actually a term now called 'sick building syndrome' and it applies to workplaces where there is a higher incidence of employee sick days than the national average. Primarily, the professionals look for heating, ventilation, contaminants, mould and so on, as potential causes. Most often, no specific cause is ever found. No-one is yet looking for 'bad energy' as a cause. Why would they? When I send in my team of energy field healers to 'heal the place', the mind-set of the staff changes, productivity increases, stress lessens, co-operation enhances and work becomes a happier place to be. My experience shows that they should indeed be considering the subtle energies of the place, because the building is full of people with sensitive electro-magnetic fields which are absorbing the resonance of energies within that zone. That's just common sense as far as I'm concerned.

Transformation of the energies in any particular zone will change the people, the place and the potentials, for the better. Understanding the presence of subtle energy is about recognising it as a 'whole' and inter-connected function of life.

I would like for you to understand that the process and experiences of your life are about more than just the way you maintain your own energy. It is also about acknowledging our inter-connectedness and realising that you pour your energies out into the World and they bear influence. Similarly, the external energies flow into you and are absorbed on all levels.

The first step in understanding this, is to notice when there is a change in your behaviour, personality or feelings and to identify which zones affect you in which way. What you are seeking is to gain insight into which zones diminish you and cause you to feel non-serving emotions. As opposed to zones which lift you, lighten your mood and bring you joy.

It takes just a few minutes to focus your awareness and then you will begin to understand yourself in greater depth. This ability is learned through familiarity. You will remember me saying that the energy is intelligence and therefore, will learn very quickly what you are intending to achieve. If you are regularly paying attention to how and why you are changing in different energetic situations, then you will very quickly learn to consistently be energetically aware. It becomes a way of living.

It is impossible to realise the true value of subtle energy awareness, if you cannot identify the external effects that influence you personally. Over the years I have heard no end of varied stories about people being energetically affected by their environments and sadly, it never dawns on them that such subtle invisible interference is taking place. Let me give you some examples:

- "I'm fine at work until they tell me to go to the regional office, then I know I'm going to have a bad day."
- "Our relationship is all good until we meet up with his old group of friends, then we end up arguing."
- "I really wanted to have my team in the upstairs office, they just seem to work better up there."
- "It's every time I walk into that house, it just sets me off."
- "Every time I go back home to my parents, the same conversation just flares up again."
- "When I talk to her on the phone, it just takes me right back to the bad old days and I come away feeling miserable."

I could give you thousands of examples of times people just do not realise that their own personal energies are changing, due to the tone and resonance of a particular zone that they enter or get drawn into. It is bewildering to see how little attention people give to making a better choice for themselves.

The more clear your own energy system, the more aware you will be when it changes. The stronger your own energy system, the less vulnerable you are to changes caused by different energy zones.

On a conscious mind level you may not be able to voice with clarity the changes that are occurring within you. However, on a subtle energy intelligence level, all is known to you. Part of progressing your subtle energy awareness knowledge and skills is to make a commitment to identifying what affects you and how.

The reason this is so important is because whenever you are detrimentally affected by certain energy zones, you are absorbing those non-serving energies into your field. It is an energy contamination. Each zone has a different nature and resonance, so with awareness you will soon be able to identify which zones adversely affect you. You will become aware of how your behaviour, feelings or personality expression are adapting to the subtle energy resonance within any particular zone or dynamic.

This greater awareness will equip you to identify what needs changing and improving in your life. There is no scenario in which you need to settle for things just being 'the way they are'. Everything, every aspect of your life, can be transformed. The first step is to identify which aspect.

Let me share Steve's story with you. He came to discover energy field healing through a difficult time being encountered within his family. He went on to discover that bringing subtle energy change to many areas of his life (his zones) was highly beneficial.

Share in Steve's Story:

"I first made connection with Sue through need. We were always what we thought to be, a sound family unit until one day, only a few years ago, found ourselves in a crisis. My daughter was starting on a complex eating disorder illness and we needed help desperately. Having had to 'fight' the medical system pro-actively and what felt like single-handedly to achieve the right treatment plan, this process became both physically and mentally exhausting. Whilst medical intervention eventually assisted with some practical and short term life-protecting measures, there was no effective source for any individual, emotional or family support. Life was for the very first time, getting really tough.

I then connected with Sue Zange and she first carried out distant healing and then personal one-one healing on my daughter. Over what is a relatively short period of time, the outcomes have been simply amazing. My daughter is now beating the illness which I firmly believe she would not have done without Sue's help.

As the capabilities of Sue's team are so wide, they have provided not only individual healing's but we also had our former house healed after trying to sell it unsuccessfully. For months we had several viewings but no-one would make an offer. Then, the team performed an energy home healing. When I came back into the house that evening after the healing it was as though all the windows were open. It was as if I could breathe deeply for the first time and the house was perfectly calm. Shortly afterwards it sold and went through quickly and without any fuss or issues.

We moved into our new home, where we had refurbished two adjoining properties and turned them into one. The property is really old in part and again we had the house healed and it now feels calm, welcoming and secure.

I have also had my business healed, both the premises and the business itself. The healing on the working environment has helped staff motivation and productivity. This part has been incredible to observe and the business is now becoming so much more successful. More customers are being drawn to the business and the results are positive.

Sue has also been able to help us as a family through a unique group healing, which she calls 'subtle energy mapping'. This has been my most recent connection with Sue. It was really amazing to experience her ability to gain higher access. She identified details of our past and worked with us all to heal the fragments of previous activities and create opportunities for the future. Much work was done to help both my son and his partner with their pathways together.

The lines of connection between the family unit are now clearly defined and whilst we have always been close, at times our lives would collide as like most families, we are all busy doing our own things. We are still as busy as ever but there is now no feeling of conflict as we have been re-aligned within the subtle energy dynamics as a family. I don't even try to understand how it all works, I don't need to, I have all the evidence I need from the work. It is outstanding."

S. Tidmarsh, Businessman

Steve had no prior knowledge of subtle energies and is now coming to understand how it can improve life in all aspects. The raising of your subtle energy awareness will help you to cultivate and strengthen the dynamics and zones which enrich and lighten you. Those are the times when you are joyful and fully engaged in being with others.

An energetically light space, creates an environment in which people can be open, caring and sharing with each other. I explained to you earlier that the energy field opens up and expands when we feel secure. Whenever you expand your field, you enhance your ability to connect with others on a mutually beneficial basis. We enrich each other with our presence. The energy field will naturally open when it assesses its own safety in any particular space. So, energetically secure space encourages and enables openness between people.

If we take that a little further now, we come to understand that in an energetically light and secure space with people who are connecting well, the dynamics between them will be flowing with ease - open, supportive, inspirational, generous and fruitful.

One of the most dissatisfying experiences for any one of us, is to be working or living within strained dynamics. The invisible tension that exists in such environments diminishes every aspect of our humanity. We laugh less, we care less, we contribute less. We produce fewer ideas, we are less motivated, and we are less invested in the outcomes.

A strained and tense energy dynamic will consume the energy resources of everyone involved. Resources become drained and time gets wasted. If you want to identify whether you are residing within any strained dynamic, then you need ask yourself only one thing, when you are in that dynamic, do you feel buoyant?

Whenever you feel fatigued, switched off, not willing to contribute, bored, disengaged, flat or even hopeless, you are in a strained and consuming dynamic or environment. Whenever you feel enjoyment, openness, fun, satisfaction, inspired and enriched you are in an energetically buoyant zone.

I know, from my years of speaking on this subject, that it can be a big leap for people just to acknowledge the presence of their own subtle energy field. So, it reaches further to ask them to understand that energy fields are everywhere, connecting us to each other and sustaining the environments in which we reside. These subtle energy 'zones', are important, they make a difference to how you feel and function. The energies residing within any given 'zone' will bear influence upon your own personal energy. Surely, we owe it to ourselves to better manage our own well-being, our interactions with others, and our living and working environments.

It is such a simple process - clear people, within a clear space, will come together into a dynamic that will serve to enrich each person and the greater purpose of their reason for being together. This applies in families, in social groups, in work groups. It will work in communities, within societal institutions, vast corporate enterprise or indeed, entire nations.

Subtle energy life-management offers the potential for us all to move closer towards tolerance, understanding, kindness and shared achievement. If you want to know the path to achieving World peace... I've just explained it. You only need to make your first move - because peace is made one person at a time.

Them... Other People | 14

"We are designed to be in relationship. We cannot thrive without our primal connection to each other."

Our relationship with others is the most powerful influence we have present in our energy system. We are designed to be in relationship with other people, and we naturally connect on multiple energetic levels, without any conscious awareness.

Anyone that you share consistent and regular time with will have open pathways of energy connections with you. These connections behave like energetic highways. Transmissions and receipts of energy travel along these subtle connections, both whilst you are with the person and when you are physically away from them. It is important therefore, to consider the nature of your relationships and which ones nurture you well and of course, which ones may lessen and diminish you.

In my experience, people are rarely aware of just how much others influence feelings, thoughts, actions and potentials. It is very obvious if someone is 'in with the wrong crowd' and behaving in a less virtuous manner than is truly their nature. However, you wouldn't stop to assess your situation if you are generally surrounded by fairly decent, friendly and familiar people.

By human nature, we weave intricate connections with people that are designed to meet inner needs, perhaps reveal or heal wounds, and drive forward our personal agendas and intentions for life. As such, the energetic tone and essence that we pour into each connection with another is powerful and influential. You are affecting the people you are in relationship with and they are affecting you.

Relationships that enhance our spirit, bring joy, kinship, shared caring and nurturing, will always feed and strengthen your energy system. Laughing and sharing together, in friendship and love, is always good for the soul.

In the subtle energy system there are two primary ways we connect to each other. The first is through fine threads of energetic light that appear like cords connecting between two people. I refer to these as 'energy cordings' and they usually connect to the energy system of each person by way of the energy centres (chakras).

The second way, is through dynamics, which I have outlined in the previous chapter. Dynamic connections are very powerful and the primary ones exist where we share common purpose with others. In the energy system, dynamics connect into the Core Centre of your energy as direct flowing lines of energy.

The primary dynamic you reside within is the family dynamic, which consists of you, parents, siblings, your children and other close family members. You extend that family dynamic when you marry and energetically, marriage actually brings two family dynamics together. Some of the most difficult dynamics are created when parents separate and then join with a new partner who already has their own children. Step families are complex energy dynamics.

Further secondary dynamics will build within your energy whenever you join in shared purpose with others and invest your time and resources with them to fulfil that purpose. Such dynamics may include your close circle of friends, work colleagues who work on projects with you, and any other team environment that is driven by a motivating purpose or cause.

Those two ways of connecting - cording and dynamic - provide fine communication threads of invisible subtle information and data about each other's feelings, intentions, needs and difficulties. On a subtle level, we are constantly communicating with each other.

Energy cordings need to be strong, vibrant and balanced

The fine energy threads which join people together as 'cordings' initiate through shared communion - two people needing or wanting to exchange life experience with each other. They literally are fine threads of consciousness directly joining two peoples' energy systems.

The cordings build from the substance of the energy essence that two people transmit to and receive from, each other. The cording initiates and/or terminates in the energy centre (chakra) holding the resonant energy that is in accordance with their transmissions and receipts.

So, for example, we would expect to see cordings between a mother and child connected heart to heart because they love each other. Then, sacral centre to sacral, because they nurture each other. Perhaps, throat to throat if they communicate well, and so on. In the case of two lovers, we would expect to see cordings heart to heart, throat to throat, face to face, maybe solar plexus to solar plexus if they think alike, and base centre to base, which is the centre for sexual connection.

The processing and resonance within each energy centre is both complex and variable. A brief outline is provided over the page on Picture 10, to help you understand where your cording connections may be for any particular person you are in relationship with. The energy resonance you share with another initiates and pours forth from the appropriate energy centre. It then literally weaves a like-for-like connection to the other person by way of the cording.

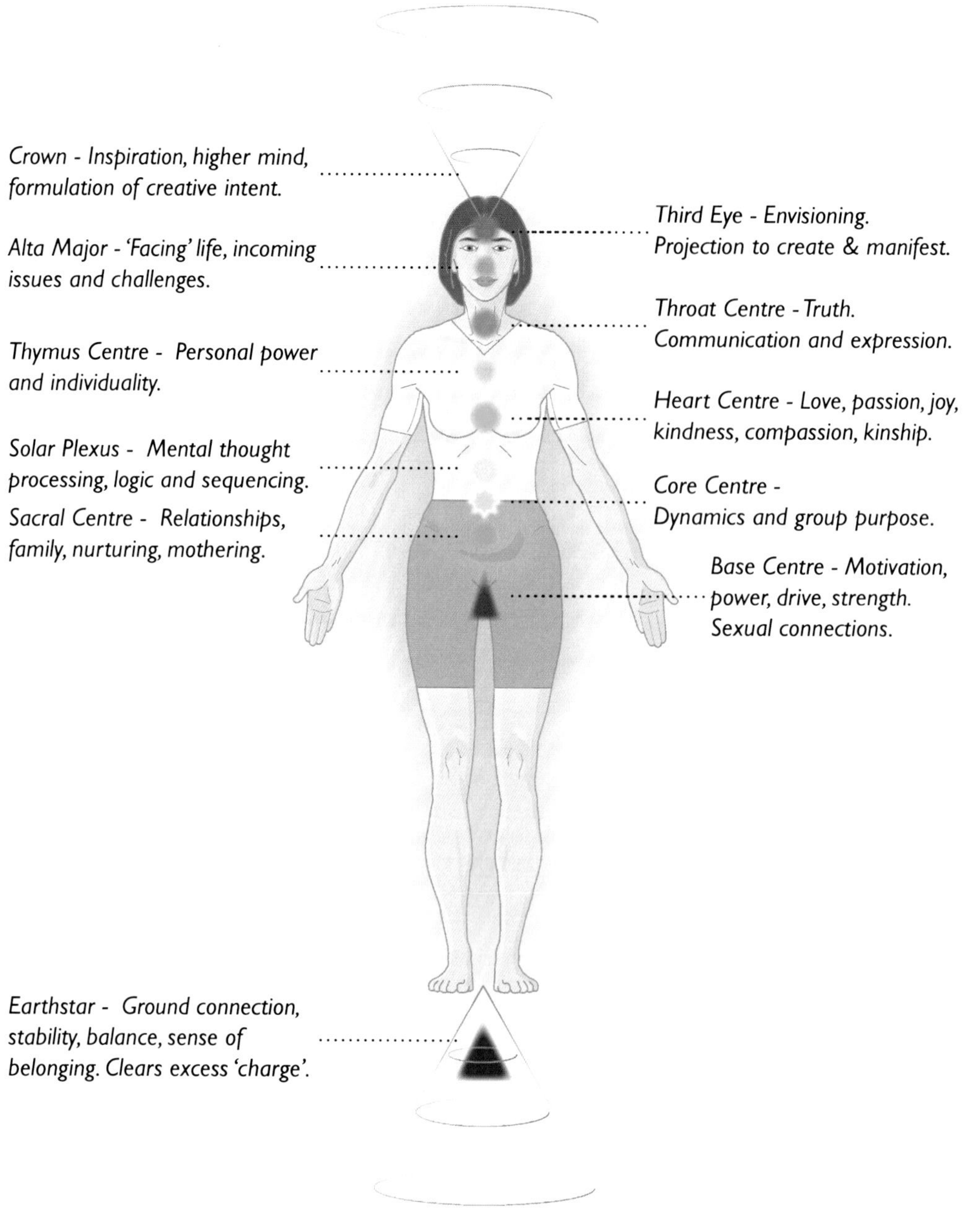

Crown - Inspiration, higher mind, formulation of creative intent.

Third Eye - Envisioning. Projection to create & manifest.

Alta Major - 'Facing' life, incoming issues and challenges.

Throat Centre - Truth. Communication and expression.

Thymus Centre - Personal power and individuality.

Heart Centre - Love, passion, joy, kindness, compassion, kinship.

Solar Plexus - Mental thought processing, logic and sequencing.

Core Centre - Dynamics and group purpose.

Sacral Centre - Relationships, family, nurturing, mothering.

Base Centre - Motivation, power, drive, strength. Sexual connections.

Earthstar - Ground connection, stability, balance, sense of belonging. Clears excess 'charge'.

Picture 10 - Energy Centres (Chakras) and their Resonant Purpose

What matters, is that the cordings are strong, vibrant and balanced. If they are imbalanced, for example, connected solar plexus (mental processing) on one person, but joining the heart (feeling energy) in the other, this will mean that a resonance of energy between them is flowing in discordance. We find imbalanced cordings occur when relationships are deteriorating and breaking down. The energetic imbalances aggravate the deteriorating situation, and miscommunication and misunderstanding is created.

I have supported hundreds of clients through relationship difficulties, break-up or divorce. The distress and imbalances that occur within the energy system in such situations are considerable. In 'energy vision' it is like looking at multiple energy highways all scrambled up and disarranged into a state of disorder.

If we can clear and rebalance some of that scrambled activity, then the people involved may find a way to understand each other, find resolution and maybe even reconcile. They may certainly find an amicable way to move forward without hurting each other further.

Energy cordings are powerful highways of togetherness. When they break down, for whatever reason, they thrust us into emotional turmoil and distress.

Struggling and disharmonious relationships need attention

Greater awareness, understanding and consideration needs to be applied to any relationship in which you struggle. I refer to relationships where conflict, resentment, or misunderstanding exists, or where miscommunication causes arguments, friction or inner emotional stress. These relationships are the ones that will consume your energy resources and create a dense flow within your system. There is considerable complexity within the energetic connections of each relationship. We are all constantly affected by the nature and essence of the energy transactions that move along the 'other people' highways.

Wherever a relationship is troubled, the connecting cordings or dynamics may flow with discordant energy. This means you may be receiving a flow of non-serving energy from that person. It may also mean the content of your transmissions to the other person is feeding them non-serving energy. A troubled relationship where neither party seek resolution and rebalance, will ultimately be detrimental to both.

When poor quality energy flows exist in relationship cordings, it is recognisable by your adaptive behaviours - when you're not being true to yourself. It is important to become aware of the instances when you say or enact things that are not in accord with your inner values or beliefs. Be aware of when you are acting unfairly or unkindly. Perhaps there are times when you say things that are hurtful or belittling. Maybe the other person's words are hurtful to you, so you react in similar manner.

Consider times when you go along with the ideas of another, even though you may not be truly in support of them. Perhaps you agree to things you would rather not. You should always take notice of situations where you feel uneasy, upset or internally stressed at the interactions, because this is the energy telling you something is not right. Your intelligent intuitive sense will be trying to show you when the subtle energy flows are discordant and/or non-serving, and you need to take notice.

The energies of relationships are the subject of Book 2 of this series of subtle energy awareness guides. The complex nature of how we exchange energy between each other commands a closer and more intelligent study. I do want to introduce an overview to you here though, because I want you to get started straight away at improving your life with energy awareness.

You have a 'primary arena' of relationships, which consists of the people closest to you, your loves, your family and so on. You also have a 'secondary arena' of relationships, which are people who are slightly less at the core of your life, but still significant to it's flow. This may be your social circle of friends, or perhaps other relatives.

We are involved also in multiple relationships of lesser priority and significance in life. Transactions that occur within this 'outer arena' can still affect your state of well-being, stress levels and peace of mind. For example, the quality of your interactions with a work colleague who sits next to you in the office. They are not a particularly significant relationship in your life, but their regular and immediate proximity will mean you are affected by their actions, words, moods and so on.

A similar case exists if there is something at stake which is of value to you, for example, your relationship with your employer or manager. That person holds the power over your job, work happiness and/or livelihood. So their energetic effect on you is subtle, but powerful.

Consider your work relationships and who annoys you or triggers your issues. How do you feel when that occurs? How do you respond or react to that person?

Consider your friendships and the times you come away from interactions with friends feeling more low or unclear than you did before seeing them. Is this particularly so when there are a group of you? Do you find you have a better quality experience with a friend on a one-to-one basis (energy cordings)? Or does it work better in a group environment (energy dynamics)?

Applying energy awareness will help you to assess and analyse your interactions in order to understand what is serving and what is not. It will also help you make decisions about which relationships to keep active in your life and which may be better to release.

You are most powerfully affected by those you are in close relationship with. Those people are more important to you. Your heartfelt love and investment in sharing their life may be vital to you. When these relationships become troubled, the impact in the energy system can be immense. In such close relationships there will be a construct of multiple energy cordings, so the two-way interactions in the subtle energy are considerable.

Energy interactions with close family members can be particularly complex and even highly charged, because they are based on years of experience with each other. People tend to pay less attention to the familiar and your family are exactly that, familiar. Do you experience regular misunderstandings with family members, or maybe make excuses for their behaviours? Perhaps there is someone that stirs you so much, you actually try to avoid them? How many times do you make up little stories, or even lies, to get what you want out of a situation with a family member? Think about it.

The nature of a relationship becomes a blend of all the energy interactions that have taken place between you. The energy cordings or dynamics are resonating with all the vibrations of how you are with each other, how you have behaved towards each other in the past, and what your desires and intentions are for the future of the relationship. With family members this can be years worth of interactions. The subtle energy essence is there between you constantly and you are affecting each other based on its presence.

It's essential to become aware of how others affect you

Do you recall occasions when you've come away from a situation thinking 'Why did I say that?' or 'It's not like me to treat someone like that', or 'I can't believe I let them get away with that!'. Do you recognise any of those? These are the times when you are influenced by other subtle energy factors. That could be a reaction to the resonance of the dynamic or the state of the cordings. It could also be a reaction to the underlying agenda or overpowering will of another.

That person has likely stirred up the energies within you, such that they have burst out to the surface without your command. In such situations, you may need to consider:

1. Has the person triggered dormant emotional issues within you, which are not necessarily to do with them?
2. Has the person triggered dormant emotions or issues that have been created previously within your interactions with them?
3. Has the person tried to manipulate or overpower your own will and you have 'fought' in response?
4. Has the person spoken or acted in violation of your own moral or value code and so, you have reacted in defence?
5. Has the person devalued, disrespected or diminished your own sense of self and you are now trying to cope with that emotional impact?
6. Are you upset because you didn't gain the outcome you desired, or your own agenda was not met?

We have that power over each other. When energies surge through cordings or dynamics, an immense amount of energy charge is activated. Dormant forms become active and emotional distress ensues. In such situations it is only your ability of command and balanced energy state that keeps you stable and clear. The moment you lose clarity and become energetically unstable, your words and actions will be misguided and non-desired outcomes are inevitable.

Unconsciously, when energy is disturbed in relationship, you will feel 'threatened' on both a psychological and subtle energy level. Your actions and words will become reactive to the flows of energy already established in the connections. It is the intangible sense of threat or loss that prompts you to react in a manner not true to your core values. Disturbed energy, creates poor choices. Poor choices create regrettable action.

The subtle presence of 'threat' initiates fear, the vibration of which is slow and dense. In such circumstances you will not enact your highest potential or intentions. Fear takes us all down to base programming... we react with instinct, we become animals by nature. Basically, fear in relationships makes us fight or emotionally hide. We become protective and we enter survival mode with all the associated energy implications that come with it.

When people are together in relationship they are actively energetically 'engaged' with each other. As such, they create a blend of energy forms and patterns which travel the energy 'highways' between them. These forms and patterns have a tone and essence, so there is an energetic continuity between the two. That is why you behave 'a certain way' with someone. It's a product of the energy 'engagement' the two of you have created.

It's essential to become aware of how you affect others

By the same means, you are affecting others through the energy you transmit into the cordings and dynamic lines that connect you. It is vital you become aware of the nature and quality of the energy you transmit to others? Take a moment to consider how powerful you are with regard to how you affect others.

Are you a mother? Then you have immense power over influencing your children. The mother/child connection is the most powerful of all relationships. The mother's energy pours constantly into the child through a primary corded connection at the Sacral Centre. Children are extremely sensitive and responsive to that energy because it flows into the core area.

Are you an employer? You have immense power and influence over employees. How well you care for and maintain, the energy flows of your company, dictates how secure and enriched your employees feel. Each employee has considerable investment with the person/place that provides their physical livelihood. Should their security be threatened, fear responses trigger in the energy. As I've already explained, fear defaults to base programming - fight or 'hide', or in the case of employment, even flight! The degree of diminishment to productivity, creativity and motivation, is alarming when employees are insecure in their energetic environment and work dynamics.

Are you the patriarch within the family, governing the flow of a powerful family dynamic? Is the power you exude fair, reasonable and for the good of all involved? Really, we don't usually stop to consider the implications of our own position within a dynamic, let alone the effect we have within it.

What are your behaviours towards others when you don't get what you want? In my experience, I have discovered that people often choose to 'go to war' when they are dissatisfied with the content of a relationship. They want things their way. They choose to fight, retaliate, find ways to harm the other - emotionally, mentally or sometimes even physically. They want to win. They want to get even.

From within the healing clinic environment, I have witnessed extraordinary examples of people wanting to get back at another, spite them, cause them difficulty, pain, loss or misfortune. I have to admit, that this has been my primary pain in understanding humanity and its capacity for ignorance - that people are willing to harm others in order to get what they want. They are even willing to harm themselves in the process.

Let me share a simple example of this 'hidden' reality. A lady came for healing, she was fraught at the choices her husband had made with his work. She felt it would adversely affect her and the children. She was livid about it as she explained the circumstances. She said "Well he can say goodbye to sex for the next few months". I paused with the energy healing to ask her "So, do you use your intimate close relationship of love-making as a weapon against him, if you don't get things the way you want?" She responded with "Well, it's his own fault, he gets what he deserves." Now that's emotional war, it's strategic, and it may well be something that had worked for her in the past.

I would not have been serving the client's highest potential just to let that go by without putting forward an alternative view. I explained that the love-making they share as a married couple is one of the most energetically powerful aspects of the relationship, because it makes love. It has the capacity to bring them together joyfully, in warmth and passion, an act of sharing that is intimate and sacred between them. I asked her why she would choose to transform such a potentially beautiful part of the relationship into a weapon, to convert an act of love to an act of harm. The client went away considering her behaviour differently.

I'm simply explaining that people often do not realise either the motivations to their actions or the ultimate consequences of them. I would like to help you understand that as humans, we can easily fall into default modes of ignorant and unaware action. Then we are caused to wonder why life is happening in ways we wouldn't really choose.

I cannot count how many times over the years I have said to someone "Get off the battle field, you've put yourself at war without even realising it". The struggle that people have over simply withdrawing from fighting in order to return themselves to a place of love and peace, is bewildering. The moment that you make a choice that moves you away from your place of love... is the moment you lessen the very nature of your being.

Whenever you choose to fight back, get back at, get even, retaliate or create destruction, you are lessening the beauty of the life process. You are making a lower choice for yourself and you are setting up a flow of circumstances that will inevitably harm everyone involved. No-one wins in war.

You are solely responsible for your actions, your words, your intent. You are the creator of the energy transactions you put into motion and ultimately, you are answerable. I know that for the majority of time you will live each day as a caring, considerate and good-willed human being. So I would ask you to become aware of how your behaviour, actions and intentions change when things are difficult, challenging and not going in your favour. What comes out of you then?

My recommendation to you would be to take time to look more closely at the relationships that are difficult and challenging. These interactions are necessary as we journey through life because they prompt us to see things differently, to grow and to see beyond. Sincerely, I do not know of a single person who does not encounter such challenges in life.

Make your commitment to offer greater understanding, tolerance, patience and forgiveness. For there will be richness within the turmoil of such journeys that you will not see or comprehend until it is resolved. Only then, does the wisdom of life fill our souls with hope for the future.

Understanding the energetic nature of our relationships and connections to each other is the only real way of successfully thriving and developing in life. It is our interactions with others that challenge us, enrich and inspire us. And of course, it is our love for others which drives us to create, achieve, prosper and fulfil.

Invest your time and energies well in the relationships that nurture joy, love and kinship. Make a commitment to contribute wholeheartedly to these relationships with supportive care, compassion, sharing and goodwill. When a relationship is transacting in accord with love, well-serving and goodwill energies resonate between people. It serves everyone well and strengthens, enlightens and impassions our presence within life.

One very effective technique we have available for understanding relationships is through visualisation. It is a way for you to enter dialogue with someone in a space of higher consciousness, a place where you can interact soul-to-soul.

Visualisation is the skill of working pro-actively with mindful intent whilst in an expansive state of consciousness. Your relaxed and open state of consciousness connects into higher potentials, so anything you visualise or create within that state will effect change. If you are skilled in visualisation, then create a safe and light place in higher consciousness to 'meet' with the person involved in the relationship. It's a great format for saying what you need to say (in higher consciousness) and to receive from the other person.

If you are unfamiliar with visualisation or meditation then please see information at the end of this book about my guided CD's, which can teach you all the basics. I have also provided information for the 'Enhance your Light ~ Enhance your Life' Visualisation Programme, which I have created to help everyone achieve effective and successful visualisation. This Programme is offered to you by teachers I have personally trained in the successful techniques I developed over many years. It includes the creation of a higher dimensional 'meeting place' where you can 'meet' the person with whom you need to dialogue and resolve issues. It is a powerful and effective technique.

Keep your energy field clear to improve relationships

Remember that everything you receive from someone, has to pass through the filter of all the resonance that is already pre-existing in your energy field. That is one of the primary causes of misunderstanding and miscommunication between people. You may interpret something different to what was intended or conveyed, because the incoming energy transaction has filtered through a mass of 'energy debris' in your field and its nature is mutated before it reaches the conscious mind for consideration. It is worth bearing in mind that you may have pre-existing bias of which you are unaware.

In addition, the cording and dynamic lines which are flowing into your field can become 'contaminated' by the presence of pre-existing energy forms and debris. The actual quality and nature of any relationship can become changed or deteriorated by the presence of that 'contamination'. You should bear that in mind also, because the true richness and value of any relationship may be being diminished without your awareness.

In addition, the more energy debris and forms present in your field, the more likely it is that an interaction with someone may trigger an old pattern or wound. This may fire off deeper hidden issues, as their resonance is stirred by any incoming transaction. That may be the occasions when you flare-up unfairly or unjustly at someone, react unreasonably, or get upset out of all proportion. The issue isn't the other person, it is a subtle energy cascade of events.

I would like to share Sheree's story with you. As a serving police officer of 25 years, her work was often about resolving conflict, working with people in difficult and highly problematic circumstances. She has now gained the benefit of understanding her past service to others through 'subtle energy eyes' because she is now trained in energy field healing. I would like you to hear how it has changed her perspective on how people relate to each other.

Hear Sheree's Story:

"I was a serving Police Officer for over 25 years and was trained and skilled at gathering evidence, collating intelligence and finding proof in a very practical and methodical way. I dealt with sensitive, difficult and volatile situations, with many years on the Drugs Squad and Domestic Abuse unit. So, learning about subtle 'unseen' energies was not something I would ever have contemplated. As far as I was concerned if it wasn't tangible, then it wasn't there! But then things changed. Relationship breakdown issues brought me to a healing session with Sue Zange in 2002, and that changed my life.

In that one session Sue cleared away layers and layers of trauma, thought patterns, energy traces and memories that I had absorbed through life experience, some since childhood. I was amazed by the accuracy of Sue's energy reading skills. My relief was immense and the heaviness and despair that I'd held on to started to lift. Things started to make more sense. By the end of the session I knew things were changing for me, I didn't understand how exactly, I just felt different. I walked out from that session feeling lighter, reassured, loved, more 'together', stronger and intrigued. Sue had given me hope.

I felt as if my life was re-formatting - I was going to move forwards. From that point on there was no turning back, a spark had been ignited! My experience had been profound. I was compelled to learn more and so I studied Energy Field Healing with Sue. My personal journey of self-discovery and self-awareness had begun and I have never looked back. Sue is such an inspiration, sincere, open-hearted and extremely innovative. I have found her to be an exceptional presenter and teacher who offers new potentials, new techniques, and the opportunity for us to be more.

I now believe passionately in the benefits of Energy Field Healing and subtle energy awareness, so much so that in 2009 I took early retirement from the Police Service in order to become a full-time healer.

I have come to understand the invisible world of evidence and I have learned that subtle energy techniques have amazing capacity to bring about great change and positivity. Subsequently, I now see the World through different eyes. Through energy awareness I have gained insight into how 'unseen' subtle energies in and around people and places influence behaviour. I have gained a deeper understanding of what causes people to behave in states of disorder and distress.

For example, when I was working on the Domestic Abuse Unit, we would carry out risk assessments, manage Care Plans and do whatever we could to protect vulnerable people from further harm and to bring the perpetrators to justice. Many of them would be caught up in what seemed like never-ending cycles of abuse. We would see the same faces time and time again. I have come to realise through energy awareness that patterns repeat and become embedded in both people and places. I also know that by using specialist techniques these patterns can be transformed and released, thereby breaking the cycle.

On an energy level, I know that offering Energy Field Healing to people who are suffering abuse, or feel trapped in situations, enables them to make different choices and move on in their lives, instead of perpetually living in fear. Likewise, these techniques may offer great potential for the future for assisting young offenders to break their cycles of offending. The possibilities are limitless.

The road to self-empowerment can be rocky at times, it requires commitment and responsibility and drive. It is challenging, but I don't regret a single minute. I have received tremendous support from Sue and my fellow healers, for which I shall be eternally grateful.

Sue has a rare and exceptional skill set, which reveals the invisible Worlds to her. It is an amazing experience to watch her work. The true talent comes in how she shares this with others and teaches us to apply higher awareness for living. Sue has been a mentor to me and personal guide, I have seen her teach to small groups and also seen her hold the attention of a theatre audience. Her unique insight into subtle realms gives us the opportunity to question, challenge and enquire about how we live. Such awareness has certainly enhanced my capacity for life. I feel it is my honour and privilege now to serve people in this specialist field.

I don't consider subtle energy awareness to be just about understanding the change that is possible for each individual, though that is very obvious to me now. I believe it outlines a way for us to change our society, to improve our communities, to enlighten and empower each individual within that community to contribute to the greater good of all. The understanding within Sue's teachings has the capacity to reach out and leave a legacy which will inform us all on a better way to live."

Sheree Kennedy, Retired Detective Constable,
Advanced Energy Field Healer, & Inspirit Teacher

We gain a different view of people, of life, once we become energy aware. The simple techniques described in this book work, they make change and they are available for everyone to employ.

The real power you have to maintain your own sense of self in relationship with others, is the ability to manage a strong core energy and to discover the richness of your true inner being.

Subtle Energy Balance | 15

"When energy within the field flows in a clear and balanced way, we remain in good health with a positive sense of well-being."

My main intention within this book is to bring to you a level of awareness of subtle energies, such that you can start considering the nature and content of your life in a different way. I would like you to be aware that actually, there is a whole lot more going on that is affecting you and influencing the process of your life each day. This hidden world of subtle energy is driving you, maintaining you, and creating all your potentials for life experience.

At heart, I am a healer and therefore, I must portray to you the importance of understanding energy with a view to your wellness, stability in life and your physical health. The human energy system is a force of nature. It is designed to be balanced and flowing such that it may be a self-sustaining system. The inflow of nature's energies should fuel and maintain all aspects of the human - physical, emotional, mental and spiritual. You need to understand your subtle energy system in order to understand your wellness.

The human energy field is intelligent consciousness and it is a communication interface which connects us to each other, to nature, to the World and to the highest potential of our own spiritual path and destiny.

The heightened awareness to energy that is now possible, allows greater opportunities to work more skilfully and technically with natural flows of energy.

The human energy form is a perfectly synchronised design of intelligence, which if allowed to be, will flow in balance unified to your creative will and impassioned by your heart's desires. Life experience may cause the energies to imbalance, then we adapt to lesser living. We may not even realise the limiting of our own potential. Energy field healing is a corrective and preventative alternative therapy which helps clear the past, reinstate the power of the present, and offer opportunities to move forward in life.

When energy within the field flows in a clear and balanced way, we remain in good health with a positive sense of well-being. Life experience will inevitably mean that each of us will encounter pain, trauma, distress or difficulty. It is at these times that energy flows can become disrupted, imbalanced and blocked within the field, which lessens the ability to self-maintain in a strong and balanced way.

There are always signs to the energy becoming imbalanced and now you have learned how to have greater insight into this. Your own intuitive sense will let you know when things are 'not right'. If you are honest with yourself, you will recognise and validate when you are stressed, in inner conflict, or overloaded/overwhelmed. It is your response to such states that matters. Are you going to do something about it, or are you just going to continue regardless? That's the choice we all have to make.

Over the years, I have shared with a vast number of clients who will admit they foresaw the damaging nature of the situation or circumstances, but continued on the same path anyway - enduring, suffering, or even sacrificing. The truth is, we know the truth. We certainly know when something isn't right for us. Yet some of us remain in jobs that make us unhappy, relationships that damage self esteem and individuality, or homes that make us uncomfortable. We share with groups that torment us, carry out duties we don't uphold the value of, which then cause us to falsely justify the nature of our non-serving choices.

We all deserve better

Ultimately, the state of our lives is derived from the choices we make. Now you know that you are making choices which involve powerful, invisible subtle energetic influences, you can pay more attention to the quality, value and possible outcomes of those choices.

If you recognise the situation early enough you can, by choice and intent, change the flow and balance of the subtle energies involved. The sooner you attend to an imbalanced energetic state, the easier it will be to clear and restore you.

Bring your awareness daily to the subtle energy movements that exist around you and take notice when you should respond or act differently, to ensure the balance and integrity of your own energy. Live in accordance with your own inner core values.

I am asking you to raise your awareness for every facet of your life. Your state of mind and feeling at any given moment, the condition of your physical health, your interactions with everyone... all the time. I ask you to come into a state of vigilance of your own well-being.

Start first by being aware of your own feelings, how they change, who or what is involved in that change and most importantly, how often they are good feelings and how often they are not. Once you start to identify your change in feeling, you will be more empowered to make a choice that supports you.

Since feeling is your initial and primary state as a human, it makes sense to focus on that first. Take some time to reflect upon occasions that make you feel diminished, hurt, distressed, anxious or stressed. These situations or occasions are indicating the presence of imbalance and energy patterns which need to be healed, released or resolved.

Subtle energy patterns embed within the energy field over time. So do your best to address issues as soon as they occur or become apparent. Don't do yourself the injustice of saying "Oh, I can't deal with this right now, I'll think about it later". Because when later comes, the energy patterns will have flowed through your field, attached themselves to similar patterns and become exaggerated and more powerful in affecting you.

I have explained to you how time flows through your energy field. Subtle energy forms and patterns establish themselves over time. It takes only a few hours for a trauma or distress pattern to start to embed itself within the layers of the field, where it will start to seek out connection to other forms and/or 'debris'. After 24 hours, any non-serving energy form will have found a place to reside in your energy system, and will have altered its resonance in accord with the other energies present.

If you recall what I have explained to you - the key to dealing with your issues is to clearly identify what the issue is, and then transform it at its point of origin. Both those aspects of healing are diminished once time passes, because the original energy form becomes more difficult to identify and address. I know there will be times when you are so hurt, distressed or harmed by an experience that you will have to retreat and 'hide'. I ask you though to not do that for more than a few hours. Be prepared to start healing, or seek out help, as quickly as you possibly can. The sooner the healing process starts, the easier it is to heal.

Normal day-to-day living will bring you an assortment of challenges and difficulties. Be kind to yourself and in the moments when feelings and emotions are surging or becoming difficult, extract yourself from the situation. Take time out. Take those few minutes you need to clear your field (Disconnection Command), get yourself centred (Reclaim Command) and refocus your intent in line with who you truly are. Don't let life situations remove you from your Centre, from your love, from your highest serving potential.

Over the years of mentoring and supporting clients, I have had requests for numerous different scenarios in which some simple energy direction and support has made an immense difference. This may have been something as simple as a complaints desk manager who was about to became emotionally upset with a customer, who took time out to call me from the tea room, in order to refocus her; to a more complex scenario of aiding a group managing director with energetically correcting a major meeting for the sale of part of the business to an American corporation. With negotiations deteriorating and the outcomes possibly heading in an unwanted direction, my ability to rebalance and refocus the subtle energy elements helped the client through. You would be surprised what can take place when someone goes out for a few minutes and makes a phone call to the Subtle Energy Specialist!

There will be times when 'time out' is not possible, when you cannot extract yourself and therefore have to be in the foray of the experience. At times like these how stable and alert you are, together with your awareness of the state of others, will dictate how you handle a situation. These are the times when stillness is your best friend. A calm energy which is in command, is an intelligent and effective presence. You will handle the situation to a higher serving outcome.

There isn't a single scenario that cannot be enhanced and enriched by the application of subtle energy techniques. All life experience is an opportunity for us to apply our higher intelligence and connect to each other in the manner by which we were truly intended - in love.

These energy skills are so tried and trusted with my clients, that I have even had calls to me first when there has been a major tragedy or accident and I have had to say to them, "Okay, I'm with you on this now, so you put the phone down and call the emergency service, right now. Do what they say and call me back when you can." I have actually had that conversation on a few occasions.

On many more occasions I have been on the phone supporting a client whilst they are with the paramedic, or waiting outside an operating theatre, or with the family in intensive care. I have supported clients and their loved ones through crisis, trauma, tragedy, death and birth. It is the application of subtle energy techniques that has lessened the impact, eased the pain and distress, and provided a higher light of hope for everyone involved.

From my own personal experience of working with thousands of clients, I truly believe there isn't a situation that cannot be lightened and softened by the awareness and application of subtle energy principles.

I want to encourage you to be more aware. I want you to know that there are ways to understand the deeper meaning of your life events. I want you to be more inspired to be in command of your choices, creations and actions. There is always the potential to see any life event through the eyes of the soul and to deal with it in compassion, love, kindness and grace.

My mission and sincere hope is to educate you about this invisible world that I have come to know so well. A world in which alternative outcomes are possible. A world where choices and responses can be formulated based on serving each other. A world in which the potential for peace and unification really does exist, because it's the world of our spirit, our soul, our higher intelligence. That World should be granted its rightful place... at the forefront of all matters.

Your Subtle Energy Toolbox

Recap on the Subtle Energy Toolbox Skills:

Quick 'go to' guide to enable you to apply the skills in your Subtle Energy Toolbox. Equip yourself for life and enjoy a more empowered way to live.

Loving Thanks and Gratitude

"So many people have contributed to my own growth and awareness to enable me to offer this book to you. I've learned from every client, every student and every challenge that we faced together. I offered such close attention when unusual and unexpected life matters occurred, that it naturally evolved into a passionate and meaningful study. I am grateful to all who brought such experience to my path – to each and every one, I offer my heartfelt thanks.

In offering my gratitude I would like to particularly mention my mother Margaret, who in the face of adversity, challenge and sometimes, the most awful tragedy, continued to choose love. For her embrace, that was always inclusive, her unshakeable integrity, and a moral compass that remained unwavering throughout, I am truly thankful. She was an extraordinary example of love's capacity to prevail and I have always chosen to follow that as my guide.

My deepest love and appreciation to my sons. I am so grateful that now you are fine men in the world, we are still continuing to share adventures, joys and the possibilities of life. This book wouldn't have been produced without you.

To all the wonderful team of supporters around me, please know that you are deeply appreciated and I honour your presence. My sincere thanks to those individuals who have contributed their personal stories and testimonial for inclusion in this book.

I honour also, the subtle realms of knowledge, wisdom and grace which show the way to peace and gently guide us to our true light. We are, and will always be, in love."

Sue Zange
March 2015

More About the Author - Sue Zange:

Sue is gifted with a unique combination of skills and abilities which enable her to sense, interpret and transform subtle invisible energies. A natural born 'sensitive', Sue is a highly skilled and experienced healer and clairsentient. She has the rare ability of 'energy vision' which allows her to see the movement and presence of invisible subtle energies.

With such capabilities, Sue has pioneered and developed advanced higher level techniques for healing through the body's energy field. Establishing the Inspirit Clinic in 1999, she worked full time in her healing role. Working one-to-one with clients for over 14 years, Sue has gained an immeasurable wealth of experience, which has provided to her extraordinary insight and knowledge of the way of subtle energies. Sue has become a leading specialist in subtle energy knowledge, including the structure and flow of the human electro-magnetic field.

Sue began teaching and speaking on this subject in 2000, in order to educate others in this intriguing arena of work. Teaching for over 14 years, she has offered a wide range of training courses on the specialism of energy field healing, subtle energy awareness, spiritual growth and consciousness development.

Sue has created two excellent learning programmes for the public - The Subtle Energy Awareness Programme, and the 'Enhance your Light – Enhance your Life' Meditation and Visualisation Programme. These Programmes offer all the basics of skills and techniques to help people understand their energy and start to develop an 'expansive consciousness' view of life. She launched the Inspirit Teacher Training Development Programme in 2014 and provides personal training to those who want to teach her Programmes to the public.

Sue ceased her healing clinic service to clients at the end of 2013. With the natural evolvement of her skills, she now works with clients who can actively influence and improve the lives of others. Working with businesses, entrepreneurs, leaders and high-level influencers, Sue assists with the transformation and enhancement of energy flows for development, dynamics and potentials. With the ability to 'read' energy lines for both creation and intention, she works with the subtle energy infrastructure of business and projects to enhance the development of strategies, productivity, solutions, expansion and improvement. Her energy vision enables her to quickly assess, analyse and investigate any problem or obstacle. Sue has found the skill set to be limitless in its application and usefulness. Working with clients in this way offers her the opportunity to serve and benefit many more people.

Sue is passionate about her work and believes that everyone's life can be improved by understanding the truth of what occurs in the invisible world of subtle energy. Her experience has shown that people can change their lives for the better, by applying easy to learn energy techniques. As each person changes, so too do the families, communities and groups within which they reside. It is a life enhancing formula for the success and well-being of everyone.

To see more about Sue's client work with business and entrepreneurs:
www.SueZange.com

The Subtle Energy Awareness Programme ®

Discover the hidden world of energies that drive your life!

Learn more about the invisible world of subtle energies. This training course is specially designed to give you insight and understanding into the ways of these invisible flows of energy. Bringing you skills and techniques to assess and understand your energetic state, this course will empower your life.

This unique training will help you to understand the layers of subtle energies that surround you (your energy field/aura) and how these energies influence your daily life and well-being. Created by Sue Zange, the pioneer and developer of advanced understanding of subtle energies, this Programme is based on 14 years of knowledge, application and progressive development. It is a personal and spiritual learning programme and will offer you all the insight and knowledge you need to manage the unseen world of energetic influence.

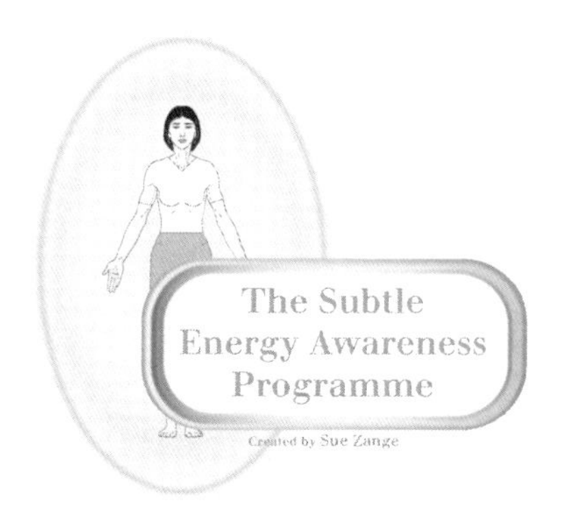

Brought to you by Teachers personally trained by Sue Zange, this training course is offered either over 2 days of learning, or alternatively, over 6 evening or afternoon sessions.

Please visit the website for more information and to find the next course available.

www.SubtleEnergyAwareness.com

Enhance your Light ~ Enhance your Life ™

A unique Visualisation and Meditation Programme that can change your life!

An easy to follow learning Programme to teach you how to successfully achieve good quality visualisation and meditation. These skills can help to enhance your life, improve your well-being, balance relationships, gain insight to your spiritual path, and discover the true way to empowerment.

The 'Enhance your Light ~ Enhance your Life' Programme has been created by Sue Zange, following her years of experience of training Healers, Clairvoyants, Mediums and Readers to work with psychic imagery and guidance. Sue's unique understanding of subtle energies, resonance and higher connection will offer you knowledge and techniques that you will never have tried before.

Everyone is capable of visualising to improve every facet of their life. Everyone is capable of meditating, to gain spiritual connection and restoration. All that is needed is clear instruction on techniques that are easy to apply and which gain excellent results.

Brought to you by Teachers personally trained by Sue Zange, this training course is offered either in-part over one or two days of learning, or alternatively, study the full 12-part Programme over a series of group sessions.

Please visit the website for more information and to find the next course available.

Enhance your Light ™
Created by Sue Zange

www.EnhanceYourLight.com

Guided Visualisation & Meditation CDs by Sue Zange

Meditations to Soothe & Energise:

Specially designed to help you develop your ability for meditation. Three easy guided meditations to help you explore inner peace and tranquillity, soothe your mind and re-energise your spirit.

Meditations for Enhanced Awareness:

A double CD set offering longer meditations for a deep inner journey experience. Ideal for those with experience of meditation, who wish to progress the depth and expansion of awareness into higher consciousness.

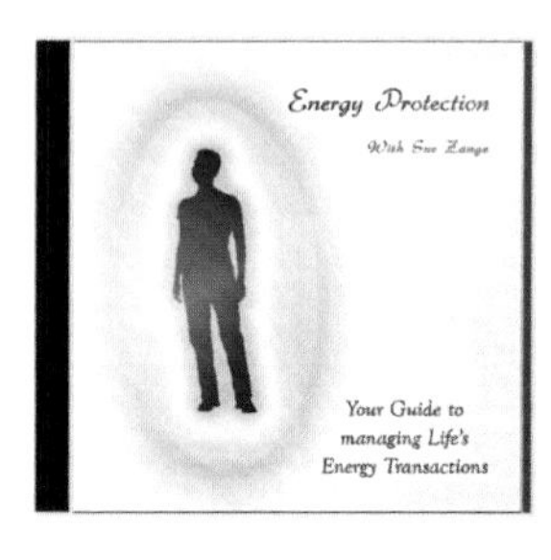

Energy Protection

Learn how to cleanse your energy and remain clear, calm and balanced during your daily activity. This CD offers explanation and practical guided exercises, for dealing with subtle energy transactions. Helping you to be calm, centred and stable through life events.

On sale at:
www.JoasLight.com

Learn More about Energy Field Healing

Healing through the Body's Energy Field

Energy Field Healing is a highly advanced alternative therapy which works through the body's energy field (aura). By cleansing, balancing and re-energising the subtle energy field, we activate the body's own self healing abilities.

The art of Energy Field Healing is a highly tuned sensitivity which allows the healer to access high level energies to 'read' and interpret the client's energy patterns and forms. Areas of imbalance, misalignment, stagnation or blockage are then addressed by applying advanced energy techniques.

Energy Field Healing is unique in its approach to alternative health care. The trained and skilled energy field healer approaches healing with a deep understanding of how energy flow and movement affects us, and a deep intuitive sensing allows the healer to transform energies to higher resonance.

When working within the energy field we are offered wider scope and opportunities to transform, because the energy field is a matrix of patterns and memories. This is one of the major breakthroughs and unique strengths, of the techniques of energy field healing.

To learn more about the art of Energy Field Healing:
www.EnergyFieldHealing.com

'The Energies of Your Life'

Some of the inspirational content of this book:

~ We are influenced and sculpted by hidden forces that are beyond our vision or comprehension.

~ The pursuance of your day to day energy awareness and techniques will lead you to a greater place.

~ The development of an enhanced field of consciousness can offer you a quality of life that is beyond what you can think, or imagine possible.

~ Our inter-connectedness within this unified field of consciousness ensures our togetherness, it anchors our commonalities and compels us to contribute to the greater good.

~ When people are together in relationship they are actively energetically 'engaged' with each other. As such, they create a blend of energy forms and patterns which travel the energy 'highways' between them.

~ The truth is, we know the truth. We certainly know when something isn't right for us. Yet some of us remain in jobs that make us unhappy, relationships that damage self esteem and individuality, and homes that make us uncomfortable.

~ Every step of the way, subtle energy awareness helps you develop a greater understanding of your life and all that you connect to on those subtle invisible levels. It's the equivalent of having the 'insider story' of every relevant part of your life.

www.EnergiesOfYourLife.com